SALES
& PITCH
LETTERS
for
BUSY
PEOPLE

Time-Saving, Money-Making,
Ready-to-Use Letters for Any Prospect

GEORGE SHELDON

CAREER
PRESS
Franklin Lakes, NJ

SALES & PITCH LETTERS FOR BUSY PEOPLE
EDITED BY GINA TALUCCI
TYPESET BY EILEEN DOW MUNSON
Cover design by The Design Works Group
Printed in the U.S.A. by Book-mart Press

To order this title, please call toll-free 1-800-CAREER-1 (NJ and Canada: 201-848-0310) to order using VISA or MasterCard, or for further information on books from Career Press.

CAREER
PRESS

The Career Press, Inc., 3 Tice Road, PO Box 687,
Franklin Lakes, NJ 07417
www.careerpress.com

Library of Congress Cataloging-in-Publication Data

Sheldon, George.
    Sales & pitch letters for busy people : time-saving, money-making, ready-to-use letters for any prospect / by George Sheldon.
        p. cm.
    Includes index.
    ISBN-13: 978-1-56414-952-7
    ISBN-10: 1-56414-952-8
    1. Sales letters—Handbooks, manuals, etc. 2. Advertising compy—Handbooks, manuals etc. 3. Electronic mail messages—Handbooks, manuals, etc. 4. Facsimile transmission—Handbooks, manuals, etc. 5. Internet marketing—Handbooks, manuals, etc. I. Title. II. Title:
    Sales and pitch letters for busy people.

HF5730.S54 2007
659.13'3—dc22

2007025095

How to Run the *Sales & Pitch Letters for Busy People* CD

Insert the CD into the CD drive. The program will start automatically after a few seconds, *Sales & Pitch Letters for Busy People*.

How to Navigate the CD

This CD features a navigation menu, located at the top and bottom of each page. Each of the following navigation methods has unique features to help you find the information on the CD.

1. Table of Contents—You can get to any point in the book by clicking the listing in the table of contents or the corresponding page number.
2. Index—You can also use the index to find a specific item anywhere in the book. Click on a letter in the top navigation menu and you'll go to that part of the index. Then click on a page number to go to that page.
3. Search—The search function allows you to enter a key word and find it throughout the book. Click Find and the program will highlight the first occurrence of the word. Click Find Again to move to the next occurrence. You can fine-tune your search using the Match Case, Match Whole Word and Find Backwards options in the search dialog box.
4. Back—Click the Back button on the main navigation menu to retrace your path through each page you've visited in the book.
5. The page number in the navigation bar is bracketed by two arrows. Click on the right arrow to move to the next page. Click on the left arrow to move to the previous page.

Opening and Using Documents

Once you've located the letter you want, open the document template by clicking on the link in the right-hand margin. The program will open the letter with your Microsoft word processor, then you can edit and personalize the letter as you wish.

You will encounter a warning dialog box when you open a document template each time you use *Sales & Pitch Letters*. Don't worry. There are no risks in using Sales & Pitch Letters. The purpose of this warning is to make you aware of the risks associated with using external files from unfamiliar sources. Click Open to launch the template. Check "Do not show this message again" to turn the warning off for the duration of your Sales & Pitch session.

If you have questions, feedback or want more information, please contact us at *support@natsem.com*.

License Agreement

Users must accept the terms of the license agreement to use the CD.

System Requirements

Windows 98

Word

All other requirements are included on the CD

*For Daisy,
of course.*

I want to thank all the fine folks at Career Press for helping with this book. Special thanks to Michael Pye and Adam Schwartz.

Also, a very big thank you to Gina Talucci who made this work especially better with her sharp eye and keen edits.

I also appreciate the work of Eileen Munson. Her composition made this a quite appealing and good looking book.

And a very special thank you to Bob Diforio, my agent, for his continuous friendship, support, and hard work.

George Sheldon
Lancaster, PA

Contents

PART I
Getting Started

What Are Sales and Pitch Letters?

Life is a pitch; that's especially true in marketing and sales. You have to pitch ideas, concepts, products, and services to prospects, clients, customers, and others. Communicating by the written word is part of the daily grind for those in sales and marketing.

Often, creating a sales or pitch letter is a time-consuming chore. For some, it is an excruciatingly slow process. Usually when someone is having a lot of problems with creating a proper letter, it is because:

> ▷ the message is not clear—the letter writer has not determined what message they really want to send to the reader.

> ▷ too much is being jammed into the letter. Rather than make a message clear and succinct, the writer is trying to say many different things all at the same time.

> ▷ the purpose of the letter (what you want to accomplish) has not been determined.

Writing the sales or pitch letter will be easier after reading the tips, advice, and information in this book. By using the sample letters, you can quickly save time and money when you create a letter.

Your letters will be better if you decide, beforehand, what you want to accomplish. Also, the goal of your letters should be clearly defined and thought out. The more you know about the purpose of the letter, the easier it will be to create an effective letter and, therefore, achieve the desired result.

Why Write Them?

The reason you write sales or pitch letters is simple: You have a message you want to deliver to the letter reader. In today's electronic world, you may deliver the written word in a format other than ink on paper. Your letter might be delivered via e-mail, or as an open letter on a Website. Some letters are still delivered via fax (facsimile), but those seem to be dwindling in many different industries.

The more you know and understand the reader of your sales and pitch letters, the easier it will be to get your message across. Some letters will be for the masses, where the audience is not clearly defined. Other letters will be for specific audiences, such as your customers who have already bought a specific product or service from you.

You should not be writing sales or pitch letters just because it's the norm or because "everyone else does it." Your letter writing should serve a purpose, and be part of your overall sales and marketing goals.

Writing letters costs money and takes time. For that reason, alone, they should not be used as a shotgun approach, hoping to hit some customers or potential clients. Rather, they should be used to develop relationships, build trust, offer special products or services, pitch ideas and concepts, or deliver other important messages that are important to you and your organization.

What Is the Purpose?

As you begin the process of preparing a letter, always start with the answer to the question, "What is the letter's purpose?" Ask yourself, "What do you want from the reader of the letter?" You might want the reader of the letter to meet with you, or to place an order for a specific product. You might ask for a donation, or offer tickets to a special event. As you can see, there are a variety reasons why you might be sending a sales or pitch letter to a potential client or customer. A letter to a prospect would need to be crafted differently than a letter to an existing customer.

As you define the true purpose of the sales or pitch letter, it will be easier to create a letter that will deliver the message that you want. The job of any sales letter is to sell, not to tell.

Often, sales letters alone don't do the entire selling (or persuading) job. You will rely on other pieces of literature that provide the selling points, illustrate the product or service, or provide technical information that the reader may need to make a buying decision. It is always best to supplement the sales letter with a support brochure or product sheet. The reason is simple: you want to keep the message delivered in the letter simple and short. The more specific, and the more concise, the more likely your letter will be read and considered.

When you include support sales material with a sales letter, mention that you have done so in the body of the letter. Say something such as, "I am enclosing a product brochure for your review" or, "As the enclosed product sheet demonstrates...."

As you consider the purpose of a sales letter, consider a specific reason for the letter. Of course, the general reason for sending any sales letter is to sell your produce, service, or cause. But drill further and get closer to the real reason of the letter, which might be to introduce your company or organization, then in another letter, a specific product, or a service.

Planning your sales letters always makes sense. Having multiple letters—ones that you can use or modify for specific purposes—is a logical way to approach the creation and use of sales letters. Anyone responsible for the creation and mailing of sales and pitch letters should have multiple templates and versions available. This allows more specific and meaningful letters to be created.

How Long Should You Make Your Letter?

Give careful consideration to the length of your sales letters. It is usually best to keep your letter to a single page whenever possible. There are some exceptions to this simple guideline, but not many.

If the letters are longer than one page, ask yourself if your sales process should be broken into several more steps. Don't fall into the trap of creating multi-purpose sales letters. If your goal is to set up a face-to-face meeting, then don't stray from that purpose. In your letter, focus just on the meeting, and don't include other reasons as to why you are writing. Consider writing a series of letters instead of writing one "catch-all" letter.

Always consider your audience. Who will be the reader of your sales letters? If your reader is a recent high school graduate, you're approach, style, and message would certainly be different than if your reader was a new retiree. Once you define your reader, determine what he or she is likely to know about the subject already. What are those things the reader likely needs to know?

Another consideration is to determine how you want (or expect) your reader to respond to your letter. You can give multiple response options (phone, fax, Website, or a postage-paid response card). Often, it is best to give only one option; when given a choice, some people cannot decide. So rather than make the decision, they do the simplest thing possible: They do nothing. This is another reason why you need to know who your audience is. The more you know about your reader, the better you can craft your message, and get the response you want.

Mail campaigns target specific markets, potential clients, or customers. You can send information, coupons, tickets, special advertising offers, messages, and other assorted things to a specific group of potential customers or clients.

What Are Your Goals Beyond "Sell More" or "Get More Business"?

As you consider your sales and pitch letter creation, consider the long-term goals of the letters. It is too easy to say you just want to sell more of your product or service.

Focus on what the overall goals really are. For example, your management may have challenged you to build a sales route in a specific area. Today, you have a major customer at the end of the route, but little substantial business on the way to that customer. To improve profitability and service, your management wants additional customers along the route. This is a specific goal, and one in which your sales letters can be modified, in order to address your particular goal. Because your company's delivery truck can easily handle a specific product, your pitch letters would draw attention from the prospects you have developed along that delivery route. Your letter-writing campaign would specifically target potential customers who likely need that product.

As that goal is developed, you could develop multiple letters, all for the purpose of selling that product. You might present samples, special pricing, guarantees, or other offers that would turn prospects into customers. Of course, you are selling more, but you are also answering management's call for more sales along the specified delivery route.

Always consider carefully what the true goal of creating your sales and pitch letters is. The clearer that goal, the more likely you can build a campaign that will get the results you desire.

Become your potential customer or client before you begin writing your letters. You know about your company or organization. You know the service or product you offer. But what does your potential customer or client know? What do they need to know? How do they think? Why should they become your customer? Write what the customer wants to know, and not what you want to say.

Why Sales and Pitch Letters Are Important

Pitch letters are the most customized form of direct-mail marketing; they allow you to hit the mark. Glossy brochures or fliers tend to be impersonal, and they are often dismissed as "junk mail" by the recipient. In contrast, a well-crafted sales letter can address the customer by name and specific need. You're one step ahead of those who just send "junk mail."

The concept is simple. Your overall strategy is to offer specific solutions that speak directly to your customer's problems and challenges. This works whether it is a business-to-consumer, or business-to-business situation.

Some of the tricks of sales and pitch letter creation include:

- Creating a good look. Design your sales letters for maximum visual impact.

- Building trust. Sales letters offer the sender a way to communicate, which can, and will, build trust with a prospect or current customer. Add endorsements from current customers, associates, or former clients. Name-dropping often works well.

- Including a call to action. Tell your reader what he or she should do next. Tell them to call, write, visit, order—do something now.

- Getting to your bona fides quickly. Add your sincere statement or evidence of good intentions to all your sales letters. Tell your reader why you, your company, your product, or service is special and unique. Tell them what you have to offer (special price, special product, new service, and so on).

- Including an incentive. Help your reader say yes by enticing them to act sooner, with an offer such as a discount, special offer, or something free.

Planning a Sales Campaign With Sales and Pitch Letters

Many small businesses decide to create some letters, and send them out. And with some luck, someone might buy a product or service. There's nothing wrong with that strategy, but those seeking a truly successful sales campaign will plan, and make strategic decisions designed with specific goals.

For example, a business might decide to use publicity as part of their plan to build market share in a specific geographic section. The first step is to develop the publicity plan, then follow up with sales and pitch letters to potential new customers. In this example, we'll assume the sales and marketing department is the same, and the decision has been made that all publicity will be completed in-house.

Publicity is often an overlooked marketing tool that can gain attention and interest in a product or service. Publicity can often call the public or business community's attention to a new company. Publicity, for the most part, is free. It can be as effective as an expensive advertising program. As the overall plan is formulated, you are challenged to plan and execute a publicity plan, and then pitch product sales to potential clients.

The first step is to create a publicity kit (often called a press kit). This is simply a press release or two, a company background document, business cards, editorial style photographs, data sheets, a folder, and pitch letter. You will be pitching an editorial story idea to the local press and media. As you develop this material, you will be working on a hook. That hook is likely to help stir media attention.

You also begin developing sales letters that will describe the media's attention to the product. Your letters might include words and phrases such as, "As discussed on the *Tom Roberts Show*," or, "As featured in the *Sunday News* Lifestyle Section...." You might reprint whatever articles become published, and send them to potential clients. Your sales letter campaign will neatly coincide with your publicity plan. As you can see, this takes planning and coordination, but the result can be quite profitable.

It is always best if you can develop a true marketing plan that incorporates the use of sales and pitch letters, in addition to those other things you are doing to expand your business. Working together, the results may move your business to the next level.

Basic Parts of Letters

It seems so basic. Yet, the basics of a good sales letter are the sum of its parts. If any part is missing, the letter is often flawed, and you will not get the desired results.

The sales letter is sometimes sent, by itself, in an envelope, or in a direct marketing package. The letter, when not a part of a package, sometimes contains a business card, or some other small item, such as tickets or coupons, which are often used to get the reader's attention. When the sales letter is part of a direct marketing package, it is used to grab the prospect's attention, provide information, and introduce the other items in the envelope.

No matter how the letter is delivered, it contains standard parts.

Parts of a Sales or Pitch Letter

1. Letterhead.

2. Addressee.

3. Opener, teaser, or attention-getter.

4. Benefits.

5. Testimonial.

6. Background or additional information.

7. Key words or phrases highlighted.

8. Call to action.

9. Closing.

10. Post Script (P.S.).

1. Letterhead	Lancaster Federal Credit Union 1 West Main Street Lancaster, PA 17601 (717) 555-5555 December 12, 2009
2. Addressee	Mr. Robert Zook & Associates 222 North South Street Lancaster, PA 17602 Dear Mr. Zook:
3. Opener, teaser, or attention-getter	Save 20 percent on all of your office supplies from Better Office Supplies.
4. Benefits	The Lancaster Federal Credit Union's Debit Card saves you money each time you use it at Better Office Supplies. Not only can you use it to pay for your purchases, but each time you do, you receive a 20-percent discount.
5. Testimonial	"You saved the citizens of Lancaster more than $4,000 last month with your Debit Card program. Thank you for this vital cost savings approach that makes sense." —Mayor Thomas Fredericks.
6. Background or additional information 7. Key words or phrases highlighted	The Lancaster Federal Credit Union's Debit Card works just like every other debit card, but with one exception: **It saves you money at more than 20 local businesses.** With discounts from 5 to 30 percent, you cannot afford not to use it. Better Office Supplies is just one of the local businesses that will **automatically give you a discount each time you use the card**.
8. Call to action	Call me at 555-5555 to get your free Lancaster Federal Credit Union's Debit Card. It only takes $100 to open an account. Your card will be mailed within 72 hours, and you can start saving money on the things you already buy.
9. Closing	Sincerely, Ruth Tripper Vice President
10. Post Script (P.S.)	P.S. If you sign up before December 31st, you will receive a certificate for a dinner for two at Cathy's Attic—a free gift for you from Federal Credit Union!

Remember: There are rules and guidelines that you must follow, such as correct spelling, use of proper grammar, and neatness. You must adhere to the conventional rules of the English language. The sales letter structure here is a guideline, but you can make changes; for example, you might want to add an attention-getting headline, rather than use the opening sentence:

Lancaster Federal Credit Union
1 West Main Street
Lancaster, PA 17601
(717) 555-5555

December 12, 2009

Mr. Robert Zook
Zook & Associates
222 North South Street
Lancaster, PA 17602

Start saving 20 percent on all of your office supplies.

Dear Mr. Zook:

The Lancaster Federal Credit Union's Debit Card saves you money each time you use it at Better Office Supplies. Not only can you use it to pay for your purchases, but each time you do, you receive a 20 percent discount.

You can rearrange the structure of your sales and pitch letters. Not every letter needs all of the elements; for example, you might have some letters with a P.S., while others do not.

Test, Test, Test

When you create your sales or pitch letters, test them before sending them en masse; for example, if you are going to mail 500 letters to prospective clients, don't send them all at once; mail out a small batch. Try about 25 to 50 prospects first, and test the results. Make any necessary adjustments, and if you make changes, test it again. If you get a good response from a test, mail the letter to those remaining on your list. Testing your letter and your message is the only way you will know for sure what the results might be.

You might try sending out half the letters with a P.S., and the other half without. Track your results. After a short period of time, you will know what works—and what does not—with the customers and prospects you are working to influence.

It makes sense to test, especially with rising delivery costs. It is better to test a portion of your list (5 to 10 percent) rather than make one large mailing and hope for the best. By sending to just a section of your list, you can judge whether your campaign is likely to work. If the response is small or not meeting expectations, you can adjust or modify your letters accordingly.

By testing small, you can inexpensively find the formula that will work for you, your organization, and your message. Generally speaking, you should expect a 1- to 3-percent result on your direct mailing campaigns, though some mailings will do better. For testing purposes, you should probably seek a 2-percent return (two responses out of 100 mailed letters) to consider the test positive.

If your test results are less than a 2-percent response, refine your message and try again. Be sure the focus of your message is both clear and direct. If you mail out 200 pieces and get no results, chances are something is wrong. When a direct mail campaign is not working, face the problem by redesigning and recreating a different message.

Don't give up after the first test or first mailing. Just because your results were less than you expected, try refining rather than dropping your direct mailing sales letter campaign. Many times, those that received your letter retain them for later use. Keep testing rather than surrendering.

Part of your test should include timing. Keep track of what days you mail. Generally speaking, mailing so that your letter arrives Tuesday, Wednesday, or Thursday might get better results than the letter arriving on Friday or Monday. Avoid having letters arrive on the Tuesday following, or a Friday before, a three-day holiday weekend.

Sometimes, the use of gimmicks can be applied to sales letters to make them successful. Coordinated with the opening stated, they can work. Some of the gimmicks that have been used and worked in the past include:

- Postage stamp.
- Coins.
- Dollar bills.
- Candy.
- Pens.

10 Tips for Writing a Direct Sales or Pitch Letter

1. Always print the letter on your company letterhead. The letterhead should have your company logo, name, address, telephone number, and other contact information, such as e-mail, Website, and fax. Unless there is some compelling reason to do so, never send sales or pitch letters on plain white bond paper.

2. Create the letter on your computer, or have a commercial printer create the letter for you. Don't photocopy or use any technology that creates a final letter that is faded, sloppy, or looks less than professional.

3. Personalize the addressee of the letter. Most small or local businesses do not do this. They simply write, "Dear Sir," "Dear Sir/Madam," or "Dear Madam." Always send the letter to a specific person. If you cannot identify an individual at the company or organization you are writing, try a more specific approach, such as, "Dear Philadelphia Property Owner" or, "Dear Fund Raising Coordinator."

4. Grab the letter reader's attention in the first sentence of the letter. If the opening sentence does raise the reader's curiosity or interest, the letter is likely to be tossed away, unread. Work to develop a compelling opening, and a reason why the reader should continue to read your message.

5. Make the first sentence of any sales or pitch letter 25 words or less. Brevity always works better than a lengthy opening. If you cannot grab the interest of the reader within 25 words, your message is probably not defined.

6. Focus on the benefits of your product or service. Features are what you are often asked about, but benefits are the real reason why someone would purchase your product or service. Always stress the benefits.

7. Keep your reader's attention. Use boldfacing, underline, or bulleted lists to catch attention from the reader. Remember that most readers will scan a letter. Make key phrases stand out so they get your reader's attention.

8. Use testimonials to establish credibility for your company or organization, your product, your service, or yourself.

9. Call the reader to action. You should try to create a sense of urgency, a reason to act now. When making a special offer, make sure it is not open-ended. In other words, the reader should feel the need to act now, or else they will miss a special opportunity. An example is: "Please call me on my cell phone 555-5555 before Wednesday, the 17th." Alternatively, you can say that you will follow up with a telephone call or send more material. (Of course when you say you will do some kind of follow up, make sure that you do what you promised.)

10. Use a P.S. at the end of a letter. Many readers will scan a letter, but will stop to read a P.S. A P.S. that grabs the reader's attention will often ensure that the entire letter will be read. Use a P.S. that raises

a reader's curiosity. Often, this statement makes sense, but does not answer all the questions. For example, consider this P.S.: "Our customers report a 22-percent cost savings in the first month of use." The reader likely wants to know how others are saving 22 percent a month.

Creating Effective Opening Statements

Your opening statement or question introduces the letter's reader to the reason why you are writing. Your product or service should satisfy a specific need, based on a rational or logical appeal:

"Free Telephone Service for 1 Year."

"You can qualify for a 6.25-percent home loan today."

"A Lancaster Federal Credit Union Loan can save you $150,000 in house payments."

Emotional appeals often work:

"Today is Alice's seventh birthday. There will be no party, no cake, and not a single gift. Instead, she will remain hungry. She knows today will be like every other—there will be no meals today."

Sometimes questions work well:

"Do you pay too much for your home loan?"

"Why would anyone pay for telephone service?"

"What would you do with an extra $150,000?"

For your opening statement, choose an approach appropriate to your product, service, organization, and most importantly, your audience.

Delivering the Message

Sales and pitch letters are usually delivered via U.S. Postal Service (USPS) first-class mail service. Although the cost of postage seems to increase regularly, it is still an inexpensive way to send a message to a prospective client. There are other costs associated with direct mailing of a sales or pitch letter (time to prepare the letter, materials, and so on).

The USPS offers discounts and special mailing programs that differ from their standard first class rate. The latest information about their rates and services is always available online at their Website, *www.usps.com*.

You may be using other methods to deliver your message. Faxes have been used in the past, but it cannot be used to "cold call" potential clients or customers. In 1991, the Telephone Consumer Protection Act stopped the use of fax machines to be used as a mass marketing tool. Another law was passed in 2005, which clarified that faxes can be sent to current customers; however, the law requires that the sender allow anyone receiving the faxes to opt out of their distribution.

E-mail is another method to distribute sales and pitch letters. However, in the United States, the bulk mailing of unsolicited commercial e-mail (commonly known as spam) is generally prohibited under the CAN-SPAM Act of 2003. The full name of the law is Controlling the Assault of Non-Solicited Pornography And Marketing Act of 2003. The Federal Trade Commission (FTC) is the government agency charged with enforcing the provisions of the act.

Don't overlook the importance of complying with the current law. Each violation of the law is subject to fines of up to $11,000. Deceptive commercial e-mail is also subject to laws banning false or misleading advertising. Before starting any campaign using e-mail, check the FTC's Website for the latest information (*www.ftc.gov*). For specific information about spam, go to *www.ftc.gov/spam*.

When using e-mail, it is best to prepare a message so that it appears as if it were a regular letter. Don't revert to the informality of traditional e-mail. Don't use emoticons (☺, ☹). Don't use abbreviations (LOL=Laughing Out Loud; ROFL=Rolling On Floor Laughing; RUOK=Are you okay?). Business communications should look and feel like business communications.

You also want to make sure you or your organization is not considered a "spammer," or someone that routinely sends "spam." Getting labeled as such will not help you in the business community.

Your messages might be delivered via the Internet. Using today's technology, you might prepare letters for use with auto responders (an automated e-mail when someone requests information), on a Website, or even a fax-on-demand system. There are a number of ways to deliver your sales and pitch letters; just make sure that you are not violating any law or legal requirement.

Formatting Basics

The success of your sales and pitch letters will depend on many factors. One item you must be concerned about is the format, look, and style of the actual letter. Your letter should always be professional, neat, and clean. Anything else will make your letter (and message) appear cheap or unworthy of consideration.

Creating and mailing sales and pitch letters is not an inexpensive method of delivering your message; yet, it is probably the best way to target a specific market, because it gets to the audience you choose. It is delivered when you decide the audience should get the message, and you decide exactly who will receive your message.

Direct mail advertising pieces come in all forms. Some businesses and organizations use simple post cards, while others rely on expensive, slick, full-color mailers. Catalogs are also direct mailing pieces used to solicit sales from a specific audience.

Sales and pitch letters are just one way of delivering a direct mail advertising piece. Unlike other mailing materials, sales letters are expected to look a certain way. Other direct mail pieces can vary greatly in size, appearance, and design. Catalogs, as an example, can be created in any size, design, or number of pages. In contrast, a sales letter is usually one or two pages, printed on regular letterhead paper, and delivered for the most part, in a regular 8 1/2 × 11 size envelope.

Even though it often costs more per piece to mail sales or pitch letters than any other form of advertising, an overall direct mailing campaign may cost less. That's because you can (and should) make smaller, directed sales campaigns. The more specific and directed you make the mailing, the more likely you will get a better response to your mailing. You can specifically target a list of potential clients or customers. For example, if your primary clients are dentists, it makes sense to target them via direct mail. If you advertised via radio or television, think of the vast numbers of people who are not dentists that you would pay to reach. Your advertising campaign would run with the hope of influencing the few dentists that might be in the audience. The format of the letter should be straightforward, simple, and professional.

Appearance

Your sales and pitch letters, no matter the format they are delivered in, must have a neat and professional appearance. The letter layout and design shouldn't be anything special in the way of a design. Avoid "loud" graphics, borders, and colors—unless they're already a part of your product or brand image (for example, if you're selling children's clothing or toys). Your letter's appearance should be consistent with professional one-to-one correspondence because anything else could scream "junk mail." Avoid using:

> too many exclamation points.

> words written in all capital letters (they are harder to read and scream at the reader).

> non-standard fonts or typestyles—instead choose to use a reader-friendly font such as Times New Roman, Courier, or Century.

> any nonstandard type size (the normal is 10 to 12 points).

> too many bulleted lists, underlining, or bold text. If you overuse these items, they tend to hurt the overall effectiveness of your letter.

Use either a block or indented style to format your letters.

Block Style

[Company Letterhead]
[Company Name]
[Company Address]
[Company City, State, Zip]
[Company Phone/Fax/Website/E-mail]

[Date]

[First Name] [Last Name]
[Title]
[Company]
[Address]
[City], [State] [Zip]

Dear [Salutation]:

Xxxxx xxxxx xxxxx xxxxx xxxxx xxxxx xxxxx xxxxx xxxxx xxxxx xxxxx xxxxx xxxxx xxxxx x xxxxx xxxxx xxxxx xxxxx xxxxx xxxxx xxxxx xxxxx xxxxx xxxxx xxxxx xxxxx xxxxx x.

Xxxxx xxxxx xxxxx xxxxx xxxxx xxxxx xxxxx xxxxx xxxxx xxxxx xxxxx xxxxx xxxxx xxxxx xxxxxxxxxxxxxxxxxxxxx.

Xxxxx xxx.

Sincerely,

[Your Name]
[Your Title]

Indent Style

[Company Letterhead]
[Company Name]
[Company Address]
[Company City, State, Zip]
[Company Phone/Fax/Website/E-mail]

[Date]

[First Name] [Last Name]
[Title]
[Company]
[Address]
[City], [State] [Zip]

Dear [Salutation]:

Xxxxx xxxxx. Xxxxx xxxxx xxxxx xxxxx xxxxx xxxxx xxxxx xxxxx xxxxx xxxxx xxxxx xxxxx xxxxx xxxxx.

Xxxxx xxxxx. Xxxxx xxxxx xxxxx xxxxx xxxxx xxxxx xxxxx xxxxx xxxxx xxxxx xxxxx xxxxx xxxxx xxxxx.

Xxxxx xxxxx. Xxxxx xxxxx xxxxx xxxxx xxxxx xxxxx xxxxx xxxxx xxxxx xxxxx xxxxx xxxxx xxxxx xxxxx.

Sincerely,

[Your Name]
[Your Title]

You can use either a justified or left alignment style in your pitch and sales letters.

Justified Style

[Company Letterhead]
[Company Name]
[Company Address]
[Company City, State, Zip]
[Company Phone/Fax/Website/E-mail]

[Date]

[First Name] [Last Name]
[Title]
[Company]
[Address]
[City], [State] [Zip]

Dear [Salutation]:

Xxxx xxxx xxxx xxxx xxxx xxxx xxxx xxxx xxxx xxxx xxxx xxxx xxxx xxxx xxxx xxxx xxxx xx xxxx xxxx xxxx xxxx xxxx xxxx xxxx xxxx xxxx xxxx xxxx xxxx xxxx xxxx. Xxxx xxxx xxxx xxx xxxx xxxx xxxx xxxx xxxx xxxx xxxx xxxx xxxx xxxx.

Xxxx xxxx xxxx xxxx xxxx xxxx xxxx xxxx xxxx xxxx xxxx xxxx xxxx xxxx xxxx xxxx xxxx xx xxxx xxxx xxxx xxxx xxxx xxxx xxxx xxxx xxxx xxxx xxxx xxxx xxxx xxxx. Xxxx xxxx xxxx xxx xxxx xxxx xxxx xxxx xxxx xxxx xxxx xxxx xxxx xxxx.

Xxxx xxxx xxxx xxxx xxxx xxxx xxxx xxxx xxxx xxxx xxxx xxxx xxxx xxxx xxxx xxxx xxxx xx xxxx xxxx xxxx xxxx xxxx xxxx xxxx xxxx xxxx xxxx xxxx xxxx xxxx. Xxxx xxxxxxxx xxxx xxxx xxxx xxxx xxxx xxxx xxxx xxxx xxxx xxxx.

Sincerely,

[Your Name]
[Your Title]

Left Alignment

[Company Letterhead]
[Company Name]
[Company Address]
[Company City, State, Zip]
[Company Phone/Fax/Website/E-mail]

[Date]

[First Name] [Last Name]
[Title]
[Company]
[Address]
[City], [State] [Zip]

Dear [Salutation]:

Xxxx xxxx xxxx xxxx xxxx xxxx xxxx xxxx xxxx xxxx xxxx xxxx xxxx xxxx xxxx xxxx xxxx xxxx xxxx xxxx xxxx xxxx xxxx xxxx xxxx xxxx xxxx xxxx xxxx xxxx xxxx xxxx xxxx. Xxxx xxxx xxxx xxxx xxxx xxxx xxxx xxxx xxxx xxxx xxxx xxxx xxxx xxxx xxxx.

Xxxx xxxx xxxx xxxx xxxx xxxx xxxx xxxx xxxx xxxx xxxx xxxx xxxx xxxx xxxx xxxx xxxx xxxx xxxx xxxx xxxx xxxx xxxx xxxx xxxx xxxx xxxx xxxx xxxx xxxx xxxx xxxx. Xxxx xxxx xxxx xxxx xxxx xxxx xxxx xxxx xxxx xxxx xxxx xxxx xxxx xxxx xxxx.

Xxxx xxxx xxxx xxxx xxxx xxxx xxxx xxxx xxxx xxxx xxxx xxxx xxxx xxxx xxxx xxxx xxxx xxxx xxxx xxxx. Xxxx xxxx xxxx xxxx xxxx xxxx xxxx xxxx xxxx xxxx xxxx xxxx xxxx xxxx.

Sincerely,

[Your Name]
[Your Title]

When using e-mail, create the letter so it appears as if you were creating and sending it by regular mail. Depending on your computer skills, you can scan your signature, and place it as a graphic within your document that you create in your word-processing program (see page 33).

Your image is just as important with an e-mail as it is with regular mail. One other element of the e-mail delivery is the message displayed in the subject line. Some e-mail programs or spam filters will reject e-mail messages with words such as "free" or, "hurry" in the subject line. The more specific you can make this message, the more likely your e-mail will get past the filters that delete or eliminate your e-mail note.

E-Mail Sample

[First Name] [Last Name]

[Title]

[Company]

[Address]

[City], [State] [Zip]

Dear [Salutation]:

Xxxx xxxx xxxx xxxx xxxx xxxx xxxx xxxx xxxx xxxx xxxx xxxx xxx xxxx xxxx xxxx xxxx xxxx xxxx xxxx xxxx xxxx xxxx xxxx xxxx xxxxxxxxxxxx xxxx. Xxxx xxxx xxxx xxxx xxxx xxxxxxxxxx xxxx xxxx xxxx xxxx xxxx xxxx xxxx xxxx.

Xxxx xxxx xxxx xxxx xxxx xxxx xxxx xxxx xxxx xxxx xxxx xxxx xxxx xxxx xxxx xxxx xxxx xxxx xxxx xxxx xxxx xxxx xxxx xxxx xxxx xxxx xxxx xxxx xxxx xxxx xxxx. Xxx x xxxx xxxx xxxx xxxx xxxx xxxx xxxx xxxx xxxx xxxx xxxx xxxx xxxx xxxx.

Xxxx xxxx xxxx xxxx xxxx xxxx xxxx xxxx xxxx xxxx xxxx xxxx xxxx xxxx x xxxx xxxx xxxx xxxx xxxx xxxx xxxx xxxx xxxx xxxx xxxx xxxx xxxx xxxx xxxx. Xxxx xxxx xxx xxxx xxxx xxxx xxxx xxxx xxxx xxxx xxxx xxxx xxxx xxxx.

Sincerely,

[Your Name]

[Your Title]

[Company Logo]

[Company Name]

[Company Address]

[Company City, State, Zip]

[Company Phone/Fax/Website/E-mail]

Content Determines Format

As you consider the creation of the letters, realize that the content could influence the final format. If you are writing a longer message, it might require a small or condensed typeface or font to position your letter on a single page.

If your letter includes a bulleted list (recommended whenever possible), remember that it will take more space to include that list in the final letter. There are always ways to squeeze or condense the letter, but that only works to a certain point. Smaller type size is one quick fix, but you cannot squeeze the type size to 6 points and still expect your letter to be read or taken seriously.

As you are creating the content for your sales and pitch letters, keep in mind that your communication will need formatting. What you say in your letter will need to be reduced to printed words. Although you are writing for your reader, who is part of a specific audience, you should consider the format as you are composing your message.

Don't Forget White Space

Graphic artists and typographers always recommend the use of white space in printed documents. White space is particularly important in letters.

In correspondence, white space is often referred to as a margin. Generally speaking, the minimum margin is 1 inch on the top, bottom, left, and right side. Creating a smaller margin looks as though too much text is being jammed on a printed page. Without adequate white space, most readers assume the text is hard to read or comprehend. The proper use of white space makes your letter look better. Readers will assume the letter is easy to read, too.

Plan the layout of your letters. Use spacing, indenting, underlining, numbering, and other elements to clarify your message. Proper planning of the design elements will make your letter more appealing and understanding.

Format Options

Years ago, sales and pitch letters were prepared on a typewriter. From those days, several standards were developed. They can be used today, but are often overlooked.

Typist's Initials: If the letter was typed by someone other than the sender, the initials of the typist are typically added at the end of the letter. The sender's initials are typed in uppercase letters, followed by the typist's initials in lowercase. Typically, the initials are separated by a slash.

Example: GS/pm

Carbon Copy: If a business letter is being sent to people other than the recipient at the top of the letter it should be noted on the letter with the copy or carbon copy reference. The word "carbon" is from the days when carbon paper was used to create a copy of the letter. Often, "cc" is used to indicate that a copy is being sent to someone else. E-mail programs also use "cc" to indicate a copy. It is also common to use the word "copy" to indicate that a copy is being mailed to a third party. The "cc" or "copy" can be either capitalized, or upper- or lowercase.

Examples:
cc: John Wayne, Greta Garbo
or: copy: John Wayne, Greta Garbo

Enclosures: If the letter sender is including additional documents with the correspondence, such as a resume, brochure, or price list, an enclosure notation is used to indicate that they are included with the letter. Enclosures should also be mentioned in the body of the letter. The word enclosure, or the abbreviation "enc" is used to indicate when an enclosure is included with the correspondence.

Examples:
Enclosure or Enc: Product Brochure

The previous optional items are always placed at the end of a letter, following the signature. The following illustration demonstrates the proper sequence of the typist's initials, copy, and enclosure indications. For a signature you can use:

Sincerely yours,

Fred T. Root
Vice President, Sales

FTR/gs

Copy: Sally Tree, District Sales Manager

Enc: Price List

Letter Production

Part of the process of creating the sales letter is the mechanical process of how your letters will be produced. During the initial stage, you will use any number of tools to prepare the letter. Most people use a word processor, but you could use pencil and paper to write the copy for your direct mail letter.

Somewhere in the process, you should consider how your letters will be reproduced. In some instances, a member of a sales force prepares letters individually. They are customized letters used as part of the ongoing sales effort.

Other letters are mass-produced. Some are generated by mail-merge features within a word-processing program or a contact management program. A database of prospects or customers is maintained in a computer database. When using the merge feature, the computer automatically places the name, company, address, and other information into the letters. After the merge has been completed, the letters are printed by a laser printer on to letterhead stationery.

The letters might also be prepared by a commercial mailing house. For a large mailing, it often makes sense to contract this service. A mail house can fold, collate, stuff, label, and get your mailing completed, all in accordance with the current U.S. postal regulations.

Knowing beforehand how the letters will be produced might help you determine the required formatting. It may also help with the design process. For example, if you will be printing the final letter on a color laser printer, you might want to make a testimonial paragraph stand out by printing it in a maroon color.

Official USPS Abbreviations

Be sure to address your mail by using the official United States Postal Service's abbreviations. Proper use of abbreviations assists in getting your correspondence delivered. The following is the approved list from the USPS:

State Abbreviations

State/Possession	Abbreviation	State/Possession	Abbreviation
Alabama	AL	Missouri	MO
Alaska	AK	Montana	MT
American Samoa	AS	Nebraska	NE
Arizona	AZ	Nevada	NV
Arkansas	AR	New Hampshire	NH
California	CA	New Jersey	NJ
Colorado	CO	New Mexico	NM
Connecticut	CT	New York	NY
Delaware	DE	North Carolina	NC
District of Columbia	DC	North Dakota	ND
Federated States of Micronesia	FM	Northern Mariana Islands	MP
Florida	FL	Ohio	OH
Georgia	GA	Oklahoma	OK
Guam	GU	Oregon	OR
Hawaii	HI	Palau	PW
Idaho	ID	Pennsylvania	PA
Illinois	IL	Puerto Rico	PR
Indiana	IN	Rhode Island	RI
Iowa	IA	South Carolina	SC
Kansas	KS	South Dakota	SD
Kentucky	KY	Tennessee	TN
Louisiana	LA	Texas	TX
Maine	ME	Utah	UT
Marshall Islands	MH	Vermont	VT
Maryland	MD	Virgin Islands	VI
Massachusetts	MA	Virginia	VA
Michigan	MI	Washington	WA
Minnesota	MN	West Virginia	WV
Mississippi	MS	Wisconsin	WI
		Wyoming	WY

Military "State"	Abbreviation	Military "State"	Abbreviation
Armed Forces Africa	AE	Armed Forces Europe	AE
Armed Forces Americas (except Canada)	AA	Armed Forces Middle East	AE
Armed Forces Canada	AE	Armed Forces Pacific	AP

Street Suffixes

Primary Street Suffix Name	Commonly Used Street Suffix or Abbreviation Suffix	Postal Service Standard Suffix Abbreviation	Primary Street Suffix Name	Commonly Used Street Suffix or Abbreviation Suffix	Postal Service Standard Suffix Abbreviation
Alley	ALLEE	ALY	Bend	BND	BND
Alley	ALLEY	ALY	Bluff	BLF	BLF
Alley	ALLY	ALY	Bluff	BLUF	BLF
Alley	ALY	ALY	Bluff	BLUFF	BLF
Annex	ANEX	ANX	Bluffs	BLUFFS	BLFS
Annex	ANNEX	ANX	Bottom	BOT	BTM
Annex	ANNX	ANX	Bottom	BOTTM	BTM
Annex	ANX	ANX	Bottom	BOTTOM	BTM
Arcade	ARC	ARC	Bottom	BTM	BTM
Arcade	ARCADE	ARC	Boulevard	BLVD	BLVD
Avenue	AV	AVE	Boulevard	BOUL	BLVD
Avenue	AVE	AVE	Boulevard	BOULEVARD	BLVD
Avenue	AVEN	AVE	Boulevard	BOULV	BLVD
Avenue	AVENU	AVE	Branch	BR	BR
Avenue	AVENUE	AVE	Branch	BRANCH	BR
Avenue	AVN	AVE	Branch	BRNCH	BR
Avenue	AVNUE	AVE	Bridge	BRDGE	BRG
Bayoo	BAYOO	BYU	Bridge	BRG	BRG
Bayoo	BAYOU	BYU	Bridge	BRIDGE	BRG
Beach	BCH	BCH	Brook	BRK	BRK
Beach	BEACH	BCH	Brook	BROOK	BRK
Bend	BEND	BND	Brooks	BROOKS	BRKS

Primary Street Suffix Name	Commonly Used Street Suffix or Abbreviation Suffix	Postal Service Standard Suffix Abbreviation	Primary Street Suffix Name	Commonly Used Street Suffix or Abbreviation Suffix	Postal Service Standard Suffix Abbreviation
Burg	BURG	BG	Circle	CIRCLE	CIR
Burgs	BURGS	BGS	Circle	CRCL	CIR
Bypass	BYP	BYP	Circle	CRCLE	CIR
Bypass	BYPA	BYP	Circle	CIRCLES	CIRS
Bypass	BYPAS	BYP	Cliff	CLF	CLF
Bypass	BYPASS	BYP	Cliff	CLIFF	CLF
Bypass	BYPS	BYP	Cliffs	CLFS	CLFS
Camp	CAMP	CP	Cliffs	CLIFFS	CLFS
Camp	CMP	CP	Club	CLB	CLB
Camp	CP	CP	Club	CLUB	CLB
Canyon	CANYN	CYN	Common	COMMON	CMN
Canyon	CANYON	CYN	Corner	COR	COR
Canyon	CNYN	CYN	Corner	CORNER	COR
Canyon	CYN	CYN	Corners	CORNERS	CORS
Cape	CAPE	CPE	Corners	CORS	CORS
Cape	CPE	CPE	Course	COURSE	CRSE
Causeway	CAUSEWAY	CSWY	Course	CRSE	CRSE
Causeway	CAUSWAY	CSWY	Court	COURT	CT
Causeway	CSWY	CSWY	Court	CRT	CT
Center	CEN	CTR	Court	CT	CT
Center	CENT	CTR	Courts	COURTS	CTS
Center	CENTER	CTR	Courts	CT	CTS
Center	CENTR	CTR	Cove	COVE	CV
Center	CENTRE	CTR	Cove	CV	CV
Center	CNTER	CTR	Covers	COVES	CVS
Center	CNTR	CTR	Creek	CK	CRK
Center	CTR	CTR	Creek	CR	CRK
Centers	CENTERS	CTRS	Creek	CREEK	CRK
Circle	CIR	CIR	Creek	CRK	CRK
Circle	CIRC	CIR	Crescent	CRECENT	CRES
Circle	CIRCL	CIR	Crescent	CRES	CRES

Primary Street Suffix Name	Commonly Used Street Suffix or Abbreviation Suffix	Postal Service Standard Suffix Abbreviation	Primary Street Suffix Name	Commonly Used Street Suffix or Abbreviation Suffix	Postal Service Standard Suffix Abbreviation
Crescent	CRESCENT	CRES	Expressway	EXPRESS	EXPY
Crescent	CRESENT	CRES	Expressway	EXPRESSWAY	EXPY
Crescent	CRSCNT	CRES	Expressway	EXPW	EXPY
Crescent	CRSENT	CRES	Expressway	EXPY	EXPY
Crescent	CRSNT	CRES	Extension	EXT	EXT
Crest	CREST	CRST	Extension	EXTENSION	EXT
Crossing	CROSSING	XING	Extension	EXTN	EXT
Crossing	CRSSING	XING	Extension	EXTNSN	EXT
Crossing	CRSSNG	XING	Extensions	EXTENSIONS	EXTS
Crossing	XING	XING	Extensions	EXTS	EXTS
Crossroad	CROSSROAD	XRD	Fall	FALL	FALL
Curve	CURVE	CURV	Falls	FALLS	FLS
Dale	DALE	DL	Falls	FLS	FLS
Dale	DL	DL	Ferry	FERRY	FRY
Dam	DAM	DM	Ferry	FRRY	FRY
Dam	DM	DM	Ferry	FRY	FRY
Divide	DIV	DV	Field	FIELD	FLD
Divide	DIVIDE	DV	Field	FLD	FLD
Divide	DV	DV	Fields	FIELDS	FLDS
Divide	DVD	DV	Fields	FLDS	FLDS
Drive	DR	DR	Flat	FLAT	FLT
Drive	DRIV	DR	Flat	FLT	FLT
Drive	DRIVE	DR	Flats	FLATS	FLTS
Drive	DRV	DR	Flats	FLTS	FLTS
Drives	DRIVES	DRS	Ford	FORD	FRD
Estate	EST	EST	Ford	FRD	FRD
Estate	ESTATE	EST	Fords	FORDS	FRDS
Estates	ESTATES	ESTS	Forest	FOREST	FRST
Estates	ESTS	ESTS	Forest	FORESTS	FRST
Expressway	EXP	EXPY	Forest	FRST	FRST
Expressway	EXPR	EXPY	Forge	FORG	FRG

Primary Street Suffix Name	Commonly Used Street Suffix or Abbreviation Suffix	Postal Service Standard Suffix Abbreviation	Primary Street Suffix Name	Commonly Used Street Suffix or Abbreviation Suffix	Postal Service Standard Suffix Abbreviation
Forge	FORGE	FRG	Glens	GLENS	GLNS
Forge	FRG	FRG	Green	GREEN	GRN
Forges	FORGES	FRGS	Green	GRN	GRN
Fork	FORK	FRK	Greens	GREENS	GRNS
Fork	FRK	FRK	Grove	GROV	GRV
Forks	FORKS	FRKS	Grove	GROVE	GRV
Forks	FRKS	FRKS	Grove	GRV	GRV
Fort	FORT	FT	Groves	GROVES	GRVS
Fort	FRT	FT	Harbor	HARB	HBR
Fort	FT	FT	Harbor	HARBOR	HBR
Freeway	FREEWAY	FWY	Harbor	HARBR	HBR
Freeway	FREEWY	FWY	Harbor	HBR	HBR
Freeway	FRWAY	FWY	Harbor	HRBOR	HBR
Freeway	FRWY	FWY	Harbors	HARBORS	HBRS
Freeway	FWY	FWY	Haven	HAVEN	HVN
Garden	GARDEN	GDN	Haven	HAVN	HVN
Garden	GARDN	GDN	Haven	HVN	HVN
Garden	GDN	GDN	Heights	HEIGHT	HTS
Garden	GRDEN	GDN	Heights	HEIGHTS	HTS
Garden	GRDN	GDN	Heights	HGTS	HTS
Gardens	GARDENS	GDNS	Heights	HT	HTS
Gardens	GDNS	GDNS	Heights	HTS	HTS
Gardens	GRDNS	GDNS	Highway	HIGHWAY	HWY
Gateway	GATEWAY	GTWY	Highway	HIGHWY	HWY
Gateway	GATEWY	GTWY	Highway	HIWAY	HWY
Gateway	GATWAY	GTWY	Highway	HIWY	HWY
Gateway	GTWAY	GTWY	Highway	HWAY	HWY
Gateway	GTWY	GTWY	Highway	HWY	HWY
Glen	GLEN	GLN	Hill	HILL	HL
Glen	GLN	GLN	Hill	HL	HL

Primary Street Suffix Name	Commonly Used Street Suffix or Abbreviation Suffix	Postal Service Standard Suffix Abbreviation	Primary Street Suffix Name	Commonly Used Street Suffix or Abbreviation Suffix	Postal Service Standard Suffix Abbreviation
Hills	HILLS	HLS	Knoll	KNL	KNL
Hills	HLS	HLS	Knoll	KNOL	KNL
Hollow	HLLW	HOLW	Knoll	KNOLL	KNL
Hollow	HOLLOW	HOLW	Knolls	KNLS	KNLS
Hollow	HOLLOWS	HOLW	Knolls	KNOLLS	KNLS
Hollow	HOLW	HOLW	Lake	LAKE	LK
Hollow	HOLWS	HOLW	Lake	LK	LK
Inlet	INLET	INLT	Lakes	LAKES	LKS
Inlet	INLT	INLT	Lakes	LKS	LKS
Island	IS	IS	Land	LAND	LAND
Island	ISLAND	IS	Landing	LANDING	LNDG
Island	ISLND	IS	Landing	LNDG	LNDG
Islands	ISLANDS	ISS	Landing	LNDNG	LNDG
Islands	ISLNDS	ISS	Lane	LA	LN
Islands	ISS	ISS	Lane	LANE	LN
Isle	ISLE	ISLE	Lane	LANES	LN
Isle	ISLES	ISLE	Lane	LN	LN
Junction	JCT	JCT	Light	LGT	LGT
Junction	JCTION	JCT	Light	LIGHT	LGT
Junction	JCTN	JCT	Lights	LIGHTS	LGTS
Junction	JUNCTION	JCT	Loaf	LF	LF
Junction	JUNCTN	JCT	Loaf	LOAF	LF
Junction	JUNCTON	JCT	Lock	LCK	LCK
Junctions	JCTNS	JCTS	Lock	LOCK	LCK
Junctions	JCTS	JCTS	Locks	LCKS	LCKS
Junctions	JUNCTIONS	JCTS	Locks	LOCKS	LCKS
Key	KEY	KY	Lodge	LDG	LDG
Key	KY	KY	Lodge	LDGE	LDG
Keys	KEYS	KYS	Lodge	LODG	LDG
Keys	KYS	KYS	Lodge	LODGE	LDG

Primary Street Suffix Name	Commonly Used Street Suffix or Abbreviation Suffix	Postal Service Standard Suffix Abbreviation	Primary Street Suffix Name	Commonly Used Street Suffix or Abbreviation Suffix	Postal Service Standard Suffix Abbreviation
Loop	LOOP	LOOP	Mountain	MTN	MTN
Loop	LOOPS	LOOP	Mountains	MNTNS	MTNS
Mall	MALL	MALL	Mountains	MOUNTAINS	MTNS
Manor	MANOR	MNR	Neck	NCK	NCK
Manor	MNR	MNR	Neck	NECK	NCK
Manors	MANORS	MNRS	Orchard	ORCH	ORCH
Manors	MNRS	MNRS	Orchard	ORCHARD	ORCH
Meadow	MDW	MDW	Orchard	ORCHRD	ORCH
Meadow	MEADOW	MDW	Oval	OVAL	OVAL
Meadows	MDWS	MDWS	Oval	OVL	OVAL
Meadows	MEADOWS	MDWS	Overpass	OVERPASS	OPAS
Meadows	MEDOWS	MDWS	Park	PARK	PARK
Mews	MEWS	MEWS	Park	PK	PARK
Mill	MILL	ML	Park	PRK	PARK
Mill	ML	ML	Parks	PARKS	PARK
Mills	MILLS	MLS	Parkway	PARKWAY	PKWY
Mills	MLS	MLS	Parkway	PARKWY	PKWY
Mission	MISSION	MSN	Parkway	PKWAY	PKWY
Mission	MISSN	MSN	Parkway	PKWY	PKWY
Mission	MSN	MSN	Parkway	PKY	PKWY
Mission	MSSN	MSN	Parkways	PARKWAYS	PKWY
Motorway	MOTORWAY	MTWY	Parkways	PKWYS	PKWY
Mount	MNT	MT	Pass	PASS	PASS
Mount	MOUNT	MT	Passage	PASSAGE	PSGE
Mount	MT	MT	Path	PATH	PATH
Mountain	MNTAIN	MTN	Path	PATHS	PATH
Mountain	MNTN	MTN	Pike	PIKE	PIKE
Mountain	MOUNTAIN	MTN	Pike	PIKES	PIKE
Mountain	MOUNTIN	MTN	Pine	PINE	PNE
Mountain	MTIN	MTN	Pines	PINES	PNES

Primary Street Suffix Name	Commonly Used Street Suffix or Abbreviation Suffix	Postal Service Standard Suffix Abbreviation	Primary Street Suffix Name	Commonly Used Street Suffix or Abbreviation Suffix	Postal Service Standard Suffix Abbreviation
Pines	PNES	PNES	Ranch	RNCH	RNCH
Place	PL	PL	Ranch	RNCHS	RNCH
Place	PLACE	PL	Rapid	RAPID	RPD
Plain	PLAIN	PLN	Rapid	RPD	RPD
Plain	PLN	PLN	Rapids	RAPIDS	RPDS
Plains	PLAINES	PLNS	Rapids	RPDS	RPDS
Plains	PLAINS	PLNS	Rest	REST	RST
Plains	PLNS	PLNS	Rest	RST	RST
Plaza	PLAZA	PLZ	Ridge	RDG	RDG
Plaza	PLZ	PLZ	Ridge	RDGE	RDG
Plaza	PLZA	PLZ	Ridge	RIDGE	RDG
Point	POINT	PT	Ridges	RDGS	RDGS
Point	PT	PT	Ridges	RIDGES	RDGS
Points	POINTS	PTS	River	RIV	RIV
Points	PTS	PTS	River	RIVER	RIV
Port	PORT	PRT	River	RIVR	RIV
Port	PRT	PRT	River	RVR	RIV
Ports	PORTS	PRTS	Road	RD	RD
Ports	PRTS	PRTS	Road	ROAD	RD
Prairie	PR	PR	Roads	RDS	RDS
Prairie	PRAIRIE	PR	Roads	ROADS	RDS
Prairie	PRARIE	PR	Route	ROUTE	RTE
Prairie	PRR	PR	Row	ROW	ROW
Radial	RAD	RADL	Rue	RUE	RUE
Radial	RADIAL	RADL	Run	RUN	RUN
Radial	RADIEL	RADL	Shoal	SHL	SHL
Radial	RADL	RADL	Shoal	SHOAL	SHL
Ramp	RAMP	RAMP	Shoals	SHLS	SHLS
Ranch	RANCH	RNCH	Shoals	SHOALS	SHLS
Ranch	RANCHES	RNCH	Shore	SHOAR	SHR

41

Primary Street Suffix Name	Commonly Used Street Suffix or Abbreviation Suffix	Postal Service Standard Suffix Abbreviation	Primary Street Suffix Name	Commonly Used Street Suffix or Abbreviation Suffix	Postal Service Standard Suffix Abbreviation
Shore	SHORE	SHR	Stravenue	STRAVEN	STRA
Shore	SHR	SHR	Stravenue	STRAVENUE	STRA
Shores	SHOARS	SHRS	Stravenue	STRAVN	STRA
Shores	SHORES	SHRS	Stravenue	STRVN	STRA
Shores	SHRS	SHRS	Stravenue	STRVNUE	STRA
Skyway	SKYWAY	SKWY	Stream	STREAM	STRM
Spring	SPG	SPG	Stream	STREME	STRM
Spring	SPNG	SPG	Stream	STRM	STRM
Spring	SPRING	SPG	Street	ST	ST
Spring	SPRNG	SPG	Street	STR	ST
Springs	SPGS	SPGS	Street	STREET	ST
Springs	SPNGS	SPGS	Street	STRT	ST
Springs	SPRINGS	SPGS	Streets	STREETS	STS
Springs	SPRNGS	SPGS	Summit	SMT	SMT
Spur	SPUR	SPUR	Summit	SUMIT	SMT
Spurs	SPURS	SPUR	Summit	SUMITT	SMT
Square	SQ	SQ	Summit	SUMMIT	SMT
Square	SQR	SQ	Terrace	TER	TER
Square	SQRE	SQ	Terrace	TERR	TER
Square	SQU	SQ	Terrace	TERRACE	TER
Square	SQUARE	SQ	Throughway	THROUGHWAY	TRWY
Squares	SQRS	SQS	Trace	TRACE	TRCE
Squares	SQUARES	SQS	Trace	TRACES	TRCE
Station	STA	STA	Trace	TRCE	TRCE
Station	STATION	STA	Track	TRACK	TRAK
Station	STATN	STA	Track	TRACKS	TRAK
Station	STN	STA	Track	TRAK	TRAK
Stravenue	STRA	STRA	Track	TRK	TRAK
Stravenue	STRAV	STRA	Track	TRKS	TRAK
Stravenue	STRAVE	STRA	Trafficway	TRAFFICWAY	TRFY

Primary Street Suffix Name	Commonly Used Street Suffix or Abbreviation Suffix	Postal Service Standard Suffix Abbreviation	Primary Street Suffix Name	Commonly Used Street Suffix or Abbreviation Suffix	Postal Service Standard Suffix Abbreviation
Trafficway	TRFY	TRFY	Viaduct	VIADCT	VIA
Trail	TR	TRL	Viaduct	VIADUCT	VIA
Trail	TRAIL	TRL	View	VIEW	VW
Trail	TRAILS	TRL	View	VW	VW
Trail	TRL	TRL	Views	VIEWS	VWS
Trail	TRLS	TRL	Views	VWS	VWS
Tunnel	TUNEL	TUNL	Village	VILL	VLG
Tunnel	TUNL	TUNL	Village	VILLAG	VLG
Tunnel	TUNLS	TUNL	Village	VILLAGE	VLG
Tunnel	TUNNEL	TUNL	Village	VILLG	VLG
Tunnel	TUNNELS	TUNL	Village	VILLIAGE	VLG
Tunnel	TUNNL	TUNL	Village	VLG	VLG
Turnpike	TPK	TPKE	Villages	VILLAGES	VLGS
Turnpike	TPKE	TPKE	Villages	VLGS	VLGS
Turnpike	TRNPK	TPKE	Ville	VILLE	VL
Turnpike	TRPK	TPKE	Ville	VL	VL
Turnpike	TURNPIKE	TPKE	Vista	VIS	VIS
Turnpike	TURNPK	TPKE	Vista	VIST	VIS
Underpass	UNDERPASS	UPAS	Vista	VISTA	VIS
Union	UN	UN	Vista	VST	VIS
Union	UNION	UN	Vista	VSTA	VIS
Unions	UNIONS	UNS	Walk	WALK	WALK
Valley	VALLEY	VLY	Walks	WALKS	WALK
Valley	VALLY	VLY	Wall	WALL	WALL
Valley	VLLY	VLY	Way	WAY	WAY
Valley	VLY	VLY	Way	WY	WAY
Valleys	VALLEYS	VLYS	Ways	WAYS	WAYS
Valleys	VLYS	VLYS	Well	WELL	WL
Viaduct	VDCT	VIA	Wells	WELLS	WLS
Viaduct	VIA	VIA	Wells	WLS	WLS

Secondary Unit Designator

Secondary Unit Designator	Approved Abbreviation	Secondary Unit Designator	Approved Abbreviation
Apartment	APT	Pier	PIER
Basement	BSMT	Rear	REAR
Building	BLDG	Room	RM
Department	DEPT	Side	SIDE
Floor	FL	Slip	SLIP
Front	FRNT	Space	SPC
Hangar	HNGR	Stop	STOP
Lobby	LBBY	Suite	STE
Lot	LOT	Trailer	TRLR
Lower	LOWR	Unit	UNIT
Office	OFC	Upper	UPPR
Penthouse	PH		

PART II
Elements of Good Written Communications

Rules You Cannot Break

Business letters are more formal than personal letters. Business letters are a formal way to communicate with other persons, businesses, or companies. As you commence the process of creating your own sales and pitch letters, keep in mind that there is an established protocol and rules that you must follow.

Proper business etiquette relates to building relationships founded upon courtesy and politeness between companies, organizations, customers, clients, and business personnel. Etiquette, and especially business etiquette, is a means of maximizing your potential sales by presenting yourself positively and professionally. Proper business-letter etiquette requires a consistent and clear approach, combined with professional courtesy. Strive to keep all of your business letters formal in style.

Writing a business letter is not just simply a matter of expressing your ideas and proposals clearly. The manner in which you write a letter and the etiquette you make use of may have a significant affect on your success or failure. Failing to observe correct business-letter etiquette can be disastrous. By using an inappropriate approach or tone, you could cause offense or misunderstandings, and create hostility, or soured relations. Proper etiquette is essential when creating sales and pitch letters.

Rules for Letter Writing

There are some rules you cannot break; for example, spelling in important. There is only one way to spell a word: correctly. There are many simple rules to be considered when creating sales and pitch documents.

> ▷ **Spelling:**
> Misspellings are never okay in business communications.

> ▷ **Sentence punctuation:**
> All sentences in the English language end with a punctuation mark. Punctuation is also vital to how a sentence is perceived by the reader; for example, semicolons, commas, and so on.

> ⊳ **Sentence capitalization:**
> All sentences in the English language begin with a capitalized letter.

> ⊳ **Sentence structure:**
> All sentences in the English language include a verb, subject, and contain a complete thought.

This is just a sample, as there are many more rules. By not following the standard rules, you are risking the possibility of sending the wrong impression. The reader of your letter may think you are ignorant, stupid, sloppy, or slovenly. No matter what, you will not be making a positive impression. And in business, you have only one opportunity to make a first impression.

Don't destroy your sales opportunity by breaking obvious rules. Neatness always counts in sales and pitch letters—there can be no errors in spelling or grammar.

Sound-Alike Words

Some words sound similar, and therefore, they are often misused. Some examples are except and accept; affect and effect; their and there; conscious and conscience. Words such as these are easily confused. If you do not know their correct use, look them up in a dictionary. Don't rely on your spell checker in your word-processing program to catch all your spelling errors. The dictionary in a program is not likely to catch these words when you misuse them.

One or Two Words

Some words are often used as two words. Some examples are altogether (all together); anyone (any one); already (all ready); awhile (a while); overtime (over time).

It is easy to misuse these types of words, too. Again, the best source for determining proper use is a dictionary. It is always best to check and be sure of your usage, rather than send a letter with errors.

Be Careful With Metaphors

The term metaphor is basically a figure of speech. They are often used in creative writing to carrying a meaning, to make writing more interesting, or enliven the prose. In business writing, and particularly in sales letters, be careful of over doing it with metaphors.

An example of a metaphor is:

The weather turned into a witch's heart.

The more simple way to say this would be:

The day was cold.

The metaphor makes the description of the cold weather more interesting. Saying "the day is cold" is common. However, in business communications, overusing metaphors is certain to cause problems. While they can create new meanings, they can also cause misinterpretation, especially in short documents.

Similes: Used with the words "like" and "as," must also be carefully used. An example of a simile is:

He looked as pale as a harvest moon.

Sometimes, similes become overused, and eventually become clichés. For example:

He was as dead as a doornail.

Be careful with the use of similes. They can often lead to poor writing.

Clichés should also be avoided. "Tying up loose ends" or, "They're a dime a dozen" are phrases that have, through time, become clichés. Avoid them in your sales letters.

Relaxed Rules in E-Mail

Through the years, most of us have become accustomed to using e-mail as a communications tool. As e-mail has evolved, the rules of proper English have relaxed. Less formal usage has become the norm.

Abbreviations and emoticons are common. R U is often substituted for the words "are you." For sales and pitch letters being sent via e-mail, don't use the common informalities that exist in e-mail. Rather, make your communication look as if it were sent by regular U.S. mail. The closer it resembles regular mail, the more likely the recipient will seriously consider it. Be sure to check spelling, and proofread your message before sending it.

Don't use a nonbusiness e-mail address. Your online persona may be PistolPackingPete, but that e-mail address is not going to impress most potential clients or customers. Make sure your e-mail address projects a professional image.

Always opt for "formal English." Avoid slang or forms of casual chat. It would never be proper to send an e-mail mail message to a prospect starting with something such as, "Hey, What's happenin,' dude?"

The Greeting

Sometimes called the salutation, the greeting in a business letter is always formal. It normally begins with the word "Dear" and always includes the person's title and last name. In a business letter, it ends with a colon (:). Greetings include the title. For example:

Dear Mr. Johnson:

Dear Ms. Jackson:

If you do not know the gender of the person to whom you are writing, or cannot make an educated guess, use the first name in the greeting. For example, if the person you are writing has the first name of Pat, use this form of greeting:

Dear Pat Johnson:

The greeting in a business letter always ends in a colon, and not a comma or a semicolon. (Use commas only in personal letters. You know you are in trouble if you get a letter from a friend and the greeting ends in a colon—it is not going to be friendly or informal correspondence.)

Try to avoid using:

Dear Sir or Madam:

While it is proper to use this greeting, it signals that you have not taken the time to learn who the contact person is. A quick phone call to the company or organization will often allow you the opportunity to learn the name of the person with whom you wish to correspond.

When you are unable to determine the person's name, use the title of person:

Dear Sales Manager:

Addressing Women

The guidelines for addressing women in today's business world are more complex than ever. That's because several different and distinct titles have developed through the centuries.

In the past, women have been addressed as Miss, Madame (Mme.), Mrs., Ms., Mademoiselle (Mlle.), or Mesdames (Mses.). The only true rule in today's business world regarding the correct format of address is to follow what the woman herself prefers and uses.

When writing sales and pitch letters, you probably won't know her preference. However, the following guidelines can help you to establish a style in your correspondence.

If the woman's marital status is unknown, use Ms., unless the woman has a professional title, such as Dr., Professor, or President.

Ms. Gloria Jackson/Dear Ms. Jackson:

Dr. Gloria Jackson/Dear Dr. Jackson:

Use Miss in any formal correspondence if the woman is single, and if she chooses not to use Ms. (If you do not know her preference, always use Ms.—don't guess at marital status.)

For most business correspondence, use a married woman's first name, and not that of her husband. If she prefers a hyphenated maiden-married name, follow her style.

Ms. Donna Chapel (wife of Randy)	Dear Ms. Chapel (not Dear Mrs. Randy Chapel:)
Mrs. Donna Smith Chapel	Dear Mrs. Smith Chapel:
Mrs. Donna Smith-Chapel	Dear Mrs. Smith-Chapel:
Donna Smith-Chapel	Dear Ms. Smith-Chapel

 Tip Don't automatically assume a woman with a hyphenated name is married. A hyphenated name could be formed from the last name of the woman's parents.

Addressing couples can be confusing and perplexing these days. In today's world, few fixed rules exist. However, customary forms of address have adjusted to the times. When sending any formal social correspondence, it is customary to use the husband's first and last names when addressing the wife. For example, Mr. and Mrs. Randy Chapel.

Use this format when sending formal invitations for special events to which both husband and wife are invited; for example, a charitable ball or a special business meeting.

When sending to two unmarried individuals, use their full names:

Mr. George Jackson and Ms. Hillary Jones

Or on two separate lines:

Mr. George Jackson

Ms. Hillary Jones

Use the following greeting on the letter:

Dear Mr. Jackson and Ms. Jones:

Or, if you know both parties personally, use:

Dear George and Hillary:

Watch the Informalities

All business letters, including those used to make sales and pitches, are formally corresponded. You should always avoid any informality in your letters, even if you are writing to your childhood friend, who happens to be the manager of another company.

Avoid contractions, such as "don't," "shouldn't," and "can't." They should not be used in business letters. Often, the writer of the business correspondence slides into an informal tone, caused by the use of contractions.

You should also avoid slang and colloquialisms. Professional slang is also never good in formal business letters. Sometimes it is difficult to differentiate between professional slang and professional terminology.

Formatting Is Important

The actual format of your correspondence is important. The format should make it easier for the recipient to read your message. Use the block format in which all elements of the letter are on the left margin. This is the simplest format to remember and use. It is widely used and respected as the accepted format of a business letter. Follow the basic rules with regard to format, which are shown here:

{Your letterhead contains company name, address, phone, and other contact information}

Date

The Name of the Person You Are Writing
Their Street Address
Their City, State {your two letter state abbreviation} Zip Code

{two blank lines here}

Dear Ms. Person: {note the colon}

{one blank line here}

Times have changed, and indentations for paragraphs are not usually used. This is because it is simpler not to use them.

{one blank line here between paragraphs}

The body paragraphs should be single spaced in a business letter. But you should double-space between paragraphs. There should always be a blank line between paragraphs to set them off from each other.

{one blank line here}

Sincerely yours,

{three spaces so that your signature may appear here}

Your Name
Your Title

U.S. English Versus British Spelling

Be sure to use the proper form of a word. Don't use "cheque" or "favourite" for "check" or "favorite" when writing in the United States.

Closing a Letter

The close or ending of each letter follows a standard format. You should always use the correct format, which includes:

> ‣ Closing words and a comma.

> ‣ Space for your signature.

> ‣ Your name.

> ‣ Your title.

Closing words are one or two words. Most common is sincerely or sincerely yours. Always capitalize the first word, and use lowercase on the second word, followed by a comma. For example:

> ‣ Sincerely,

> ‣ Sincerely yours,

Other common closing words are:

> ‣ Cordially,

> ‣ Yours truly,

> ‣ Very truly yours,

> ‣ Yours sincerely,

> ‣ Best regards,

> ‣ Respectfully,

> ‣ Respectfully yours,

Improving Your Prose

There are many little ways for you to improve your writing. The more you strive for better sentences, the more likely your writing will come to life. English is a rich language, and there is often more than one way to say something or communicate your message. Other more structured languages do not offer the wide flexibility available in English. Perhaps the multiple ways of making your point provides too many options.

With multiple ways to say whatever it is you intend to say, it often becomes more difficult, time-consuming, and even perplexing to create good writing. This becomes even more apparent when you are writing business letters.

10 Tips to Improve Your Prose

1. Keep it simple. Complicated sentences are hard for your reader to comprehend.

2. Avoid informal words. Contractions (isn't, aren't, shouldn't, couldn't) are informal.

3. Rewrite sentences that start, "There is..." or, "There are..." Most times, these sentences could be better structured.

4. Use solid, descriptive verbs. Although there is nothing wrong with soft verbs, such as "got" or "put," try to replace them with better verbs. For example, change this sentence: "She got the package." To: "She accepted the package."

5. Write for your reader. That is the ultimate purpose of your writing. Who will read what you are writing? Decide that, and then write for your specific audience.

6. Forget the baffling. Some people believe it makes sense to "baffle them with bull excrement." All you do, with this approach, is make your writing confusing, unclear, and unreadable.

7. Don't be sloppy. Go back to your work, and look for errors, problems, and ways to improve what you wrote.

8. Understand that writing is a process. It happens in stages. You start with an idea, you begin to write, you polish your writing, it is edited, and it is reviewed again.

9. Say it with as few words as possible. Whatever you are trying to say, it is easy to say too much. Brevity is better than longevity. If you can make your point in 10 words, don't say it with 15 words.

10. Don't be afraid to start over. Sometimes, it's best to start with a clean slate. Set aside what you wrote, and then try a new approach to convey your message.

Redundancy and Unnecessary Words

When engineering, redundancy is often a good thing. Engineers design and build in redundancy. If one system fails, a second is available to take over and prevent a problem. In writing, redundancy is not such a good thing. In fact, it should be avoided.

The duplication of thought—words placed together so as to say the same thing twice—is not good. Consider the phrase, "brief in duration." What do the words "in duration" add to the description of "brief"? If it is brief, the words "in duration" add nothing.

In business, there are many such phrases that are used in written communication. They do little to improve or make your writing clearer or better, and should be avoided. Cut them from your writing. Here is a list of such phrases, along with suggestions on how to replace them:

Redundant Phrase	Replace With
12 midnight	midnight
12 noon	noon
absolute necessity	necessity
absolutely complete	complete
absolutely essential	essential
actual experience, past experience	experience
added bonus	bonus
advance notice	notice
advance planning	planning
advance reservations	reservations

Redundant Phrase	Replace With
advance warning	warning
all meet together	all meet
already exist	drop "exist"
and also	use "either" and/or "also" but not both
are in receipt of	have, have received, received
arrived at the conclusion	concluded, assumed, closed, decided, ended, finished, inferred, settled
ask the question	ask
assembled together	assembled
at 12 noon	at noon
at about	about or at
at the earliest possible date	as soon as, as soon as possible, soon
ATM machine	ATM
basic essentials	essentials
basic fundamentals	fundamentals
before, *or* in the past	before, *or* in the past
biography of his/her life	biography
blue, green, red...in color	blue, green, red...
brief in duration	brief
capital city, Capitol building	capital, Capitol
CD-ROM disk	CD-ROM
city of (Philadelphia, Lancaster, and so on)	drop "city of"
clearly evident	obvious
close proximity	close, near
collaborate together	collaborate
complete monopoly	monopoly
completely demolished, completely destroyed	demolished, destroyed
completely opposite	opposite
completely surrounded	surrounded
connect together	connect

Redundant Phrase	Replace With
consensus of opinion	agreement
continue on	continue
contributing factor	cause, factor, reason
controversial issue	issue
cooperate together	cooperate
costs a total of	costs
costs the sum of	costs
current status	status
difficult dilemma	dilemma
divide up	divide
doctorate degree	doctorate
each and every	each *or* every (not both)
enclosed herewith please find, enclosed herein	enclosed is, here is, here are, I enclose, with this
end result	result
estimated at about	about or estimated at
estimated roughly	estimated
exactly identical	identical
fair and equitable	fair or equitable
few in number	few
filled to capacity	filled
final outcome	outcome
first and foremost	first, chief, main
first began	began
first created	created
foreign imports	imports
free gift	gift
future plans	plans
general consensus	consensus
general consensus (of opinion)	consensus
general public	public, citizens
group together	group

Redundant Phrase	Replace With
he/she is a person who	he/she
HIV virus	HIV
honest truth	truth
I wish to take this opportunity to thank you	thank you
if and when	*either* if *or* when
important essentials	essentials
in the month of January	in January
inside of	inside
join together, link together	join, link
made a statement saying	said, stated
merge together, mingle together, mix together	merge, mingle, mix
month of January, month of June...	January, June...
more and more	often, more
mutual advantage of both	mutual advantage
new breakthrough	breakthrough
new development	development
none at all	none
outside of	outside
over and over	again, repeatedly
over exaggerate	exaggerate
pair of twins	twins
particular interest	interest
past experience, past history	experience, history, past
past history	history
pause for a moment	pause
period of time	either period or time
point in time	either now or today
postpone until later	postpone
pre-existing, prerecorded	existing, recorded
protest against	protest

Redundant Phrase	Replace With
protrude out	protrude
reelected for another term	reelected
refer (repay, return, revert) back	back
refer back	refer
regress back	regress
repeat again	repeat
rise up	rise
same identical	same
small in size	small
square in shape	square
still continues to	continues to
still remains	remains
storm event	storm
sum total	total
surrounded on all sides	surrounded
temporary loan	loan
the reason is because, the reason why	reasons, (the) reason is, because
throughout the entire	throughout
time period	time, period
total number	total *or* number
totally demolished, totally destroyed	demolished, destroyed
triangular in shape	triangular
true fact	fact
unexpected surprise	surprise
unite together	unite
unless or until	either unless or until
up until	until
usual habit	habit
very hurriedly	hurriedly
visible to the eye	visible

Consider What You Are Saying

When you are writing a business letter, think about the content. The way you say whatever it is you want to say is important. Consider these points:

> ▷ Determine the purpose of the letter.

> ▷ Never assume that your reader has a specific level of knowledge.

> ▷ Do not make sensational or unsubstantiated claims.

> ▷ Never exaggerate facts to make your points.

> ▷ Do not digress into unrelated issues or business. Stick to the purpose of the letter.

> ▷ Do not make your letter too long.

> ▷ Eliminate jargon.

As you think about what you are saying, again, consider your reader. If you are writing to 20-year old girls, would you say it the same way as if your audience were 70-year-old retired men?

Consider age, gender, marital status, vocation, location, business objectives, interests, and other similar factors when you write your sales or pitch letter. Some groups may be concerned about price, some about service, and others about developing a long-term, professional relationship. All of these factors should determine how you are developing your sales and pitch letters.

Say It Positively

When composing sales letters, try to state facts and assertions positively, rather than negatively. Consider these two examples:

Example 1: Only 3 percent of our loan applicants are denied.

Example 2: A whopping 97 percent of those applying for loans are approved.

As you can see, the second example allows an affirmation as to why someone should apply. It suggests the reader will also be included on the list of approved loans.

Some other examples are:

Example 1: Easy Care Lawn eliminates weeds.

Example 2: You get a weed-free lawn all summer.

Example 1: Reduce your office staff's downtime by 15 percent.

Example 2: Increase your office staff's production by 15 percent.

Verb Usage

When writing, use effective and powerful verbs to communicate with your letter's reader.

Write in the Past Tense

For most of your letters, it is more effective to write in the past tense as it is easier to express yourself.

There are some exceptions, such as future tense; for example, I will call you next week.

To help you write more sentences and to create stronger letters, use this list of stronger verbs:

Strong Verbs			
abated	accounted	addressed	advanced
abbreviated	accredited	adduced	advertised
abided	accrued	adhered	advised
absolved	accumulated	adjoined	advocated
absorbed	accustomed	adjourned	aerated
abstained	achieved	adjudged	affected
abstracted	acknowledged	adjudicated	affiliated
abutted	acquainted	adjured	affirmed
accelerated	acquiesced	adjusted	affixed
accented	acquired	ad-libbed	afforded
accepted	acquitted	administered	agglutinated
acclaimed	acted	admired	aggrandized
acclimatized	activated	admitted	agreed
accommodated	actualized	adopted	aided
accompanied	actuated	adored	aligned
accomplished	adapted	adorned	allied
accorded	added	adumbrated	allocated

Strong Verbs

allotted	argued	audited	calculated
alternated	arose (from)	augmented	calmed
amazed	arranged	authored	campaigned
amended	arrived	authorize	camped
amplified	articulated	automated	captivated
amused	ascertained	availed	carded
analyzed	ascribed	awarded	cared
anesthetized	aspired	backed	carried
animated	assayed	banded	carted
annotated	assembled	banked	carved
announced	asserted	bartered	catalogued
answered	assessed	beaded	catapulted
anticipated	assigned	became	centered
antiqued	assimilated	begot	chaired
appealed	assisted	benchmarked	changed
appeared	associated	benefited	channeled
appended	assumed	booked	characterized
appertained (to)	assured	bought	charged
applauded	astonished	braided	charted
applied	astounded	brailed	chartered
appliquéd	attached	branched	cheered
appointed	attained	branded	cherished
appraised	attempted	brandished	chiseled
apprised	attended	breaded	chronicled
approached	attitudinized	bred	cited
approved	attributed	broadcasted	civilized
approximated	attuned	brought	claimed
arbitrated	audio dictated	budgeted	clarified
archived	audio taped	built	cleaned

Strong Verbs

cleared	conciliated	counseled	deferred
clocked	concluded	counted	defined
closed	conducted	countered	deflected
clued	configured	courted	deigned
coached	congratulated	created	delegated
coded	congregated	credited	deleted
codified	connected	crewed	delighted
coifed	connoted	critiqued	delineated
collaborated	conquered	crusaded	delivered
collected	conserved	cued	demonstrated
colored	considered	cultured	demystified
comforted	constructed	curtailed	denoted
commanded	construed	customized	depicted
commemorated	consulted	cut	deprogrammed
commercialized	consumed	cycled	deregulated
commissioned	continued	dated	derived
communicated	contracted	dealt	derived
compared	contributed	debited	described
compensated	controlled	debriefed	designed
competed	converged	debugged	detailed
compiled	conversed	decentralized	detected
completed	cooperated	decided	determined
complimented	co-opted	deciphered	detoured
composed	coordinated	declaimed	developed
computed	copy wrote	declared	devised
computerized	copyrighted	decoded	devolved
conceived	corded	decorated	devoted
concentrated	corrected	decreased	diagnosed
conceptualized	correlated	dedicated	dialogued

Strong Verbs			
diced	drove	enlightened	examined
dictated	earned	enlisted	excavated
differed	edited	enlivened	excelled
digested	editorialized	enriched	exchanged
digitized	educated	ensconced	exclaimed
digitized	effected	ensured	excoriated
diluted	effloresced	entered	exculpated
dined	eked out	entertained	executed
directed	elaborated	envisioned	exemplified
disagreed	elasticized	epigrammatized	exercised
disclosed	elbowed	epitomized	exfoliated
discovered	elected	equalized	exhibited
discussed	elegized	erected	exhorted
dispatched	elevated	eructed	exonerated
dispersed	eliminated	escorted	exorcized
displayed	embroidered	established	expanded
dissolved	emended	estimated	expedited
distributed	emphasized	etched	experienced
dithered	employed	eulogized	explained
diversified	empowered	euphemized	explored
divided	encased	evaluated	exported
divined	encountered	evanesced	exposed
divulged	encouraged	evangelized	expressed
docked	energized	evidenced	extended
documented	engaged	evoked	extolled
donated	engineered	evolved	facilitated
doused	engraved	exacerbated	farmed
drafted	enhanced	exacted	fascinated
drew	enlarged	exalted	fastened

Strong Verbs			
faxed	founded	handled	implied
fed	franchised	harbored	imported
federalized	fraternized	harmonized	imposed
ferreted	freed	harvested	impressed
fertilized	froze	hastened	improved
fetched	fulfilled	headed	incited
fictionalized	functioned	healed	included
filed	furnished	heaped	incorporated
filled	gained	heard	increased
filmed	garnished	heated	indexed
financed	gathered	helped	indicated
fired	gave	hewed	indicted
fitted	generated	hired	indulged
fixed	gestured	honored	industrialized
flattered	girded	hoped	influenced
flaunted	glorified	hosted	informed
flew	governed	hugged	initialized
flourished	graded	humanized	initiated
flowcharted	grafted	humored	inked
fluctuated	granted	hustled	inquired
followed	graphed	hypnotized	inspected
forecasted	gratified	hypothesized	inspired
formalized	greeted	identified	installed
formatted	grew	ignited	instituted
formed	guaranteed	illustrated	instructed
formulated	guarded	imagined	insured
fortified	guided	immigrated	integrated
forwarded	hailed	implanted	interested
found	halted	implemented	interfaced

Strong Verbs

internalized	led	merged	operated
internationalized	left	met	opined
interpreted	legalized	migrated	orated
interviewed	legislated	ministered	orchestrated
introduced	legitimized	modeled	ordered
intuited	lessened	moderated	organized
invented	lighted	modified	oriented
inventoried	linked	molded	originated
inverted	listened	monitored	outlaid
invested	litigated	morphed	outlined
investigated	loaded	mortgaged	outnumbered
invigorated	loaned	motivated	outpaced
involved	lobbied	moved	outperformed
issued	localized	multiplied	outplayed
joined	looked	multitasked	outran
journalized	magnetized	narrated	outranked
journeyed	mailed	navigated	outshone
judged	maintained	negotiated	outvoted
juried	managed	networked	outwitted
justified	manipulated	neutralized	overcame
juxtaposed	manufactured	normalized	overdid
keyboarded	marked	notarized	overheard
lamented	marketed	noted	oversaw
laminated	mastered	notified	overstepped
landed	measured	nourished	overstretched
landscaped	mediated	nursed	overwhelmed
launched	memorized	obtained	overworked
leased	mentored	officiated	overwrote
lectured	merchandised	opened	owed

Strong Verbs

owned	plotted	proscribed	received
oxidized	pooled	prospered	recited
oxygenated	posed	protected	reclaimed
paced	positioned	protested	recognized
packaged	posted	protracted	recommended
packed	practiced	proved	reconciled
parented	praised	provided	reconstructed
participated	prayed	publicized	recorded
partnered	predicted	published	recouped
patented	preempted	purchased	recovered
patterned	prefaced	pursued	recreated
perceived	preferred	qualified	recruited
perfected	prepared	quantified	rectified
performed	presented	questioned	recycled
persevered	presided	queued	redecorated
persisted	pressed	quickened	redesigned
personalized	prevented	quilted	redistricted
persuaded	probed	raised	reduced
perused	proceeded	ran	reenacted
petitioned	processed	ranged	reentered
photocopied	procured	rated	referenced
photographed	produced	razed	refreshed
piloted	professionalized	reached	registered
pinpointed	programmed	realized	regulated
pitched	projected	reaped	rehearsed
placed	promoted	reared	rehired
planned	promulgated	rearranged	reimbursed
planted	proofread	reasoned	reinforced
played	proposed	recalled	rejoiced

Strong Verbs

related	resumed	scrimped	speculated
released	retailed	sculptured	spiced
relinquished	retained	secured	spirited
relocated	retired	selected	spoke
remedied	retooled	sensed	sponsored
remembered	retorted	sequenced	spread
reminisced	retrained	serialized	stabilized
remodeled	retrieved	served	staffed
renewed	returned	set	standardized
rented	reunited	sewed	starred
reoriented	revamped	shaped	stated
repaired	reveled	shared	stepped
replaced	reviewed	showed	sterilized
replenished	revised	shredded	stimulated
replied	revived	signified	stored
reported	rewired	simplified	straightened
reposed	rolled	sized	streamlined
represented	rose	skilled	strengthened
requested	rotated	socialized	stretched
required	routed	sold	strolled
requisitioned	rushed	solicited	strove
researched	sailed	solidified	structured
reshaped	sampled	solved	styled
resized	sanitized	sorted	subcontracted
resolved	saved	sought	submitted
resourced	scanned	spared	succeeded
responded	scheduled	sparked	summarized
restored	scored	spayed	supervised
resulted	screened	specified	supplied

Strong Verbs

supported	traded	upgraded	watched
surfed	trained	uplifted	waved
surmised	transacted	used	weaned
surveyed	transcribed	utilized	weighed
survived	transferred	validated	weighted
syndicated	translated	valued	welded
synthesized	transmitted	varied	wholesaled
systematized	transported	vaunted	willed
tabulated	traveled	venerated	wintered
tamped	treated	ventured	withdrew
taught	trekked	verbalized	won
taxed	triumphed	verified	word-processed
teamed	trucked	videotaped	worked
telephoned	truncated	viewed	wrote
televised	trusted	vindicated	wrought
terminated	turned	visualized	x-rayed
tested	typed	vitalized	yearned
thwarted	typeset	vocalized	yielded
told	underscored	voiced	zeroed (in)
tolled	understood	volunteered	zoned
toughened	undertook	voted	
toured	unified	vulcanized	
traced	united	waited	
tracked	updated	waived	

Avoiding Sexist Language

In the past couple of decades, there has been an effort to avoid sexist language in business communications. Therefore, it makes sense to avoid discriminatory words in your business letters.

The best advice is to treat all readers and people equally. Simply, this means that you should address men and women as equals in your sales and pitch letters. Some examples of sexist language and how to change are:

> ▷ instead of using the word "Chairman," replace it with "the Chair" or "the leader."

> ▷ "manpower" can be replaced with workforce, staff, employees, associates, personnel, or workers.

> ▷ "fireman" should be changed to fire fighter.

Some additional examples are:

Instead of:	Use
businessman	business executive
congressman	congressional representative
mailman	mail carrier
stewardess	flight attendant
policewoman	police officer

Change the Sentence to Plural to Eliminate Problems

By changing the sentence from singular to a plural form, you can eliminate sexist language. For example, consider this sentence:

We give each customer his rebate at the time of purchase.

But if you change the sentence to plural, the sentence no longer has any sexist connotation:

We give our customers their rebates at the time of purchase.

Avoiding Other Problematic Language

As our society moves forward, the use of certain language changed. English is rich and offers many alternatives; it just takes effort on your part to avoid words that could be questioned, misconstrued, or considered provocative or politically incorrect. For example, years ago, it was common to refer to people with a hearing problem as "deaf." Today, that is inappropriate, at best. Rather than use the word "deaf," it could be replaced with "individual who cannot hear."

Descriptive words such as "crippled" have been replaced with "disabled."

Making Your Letters Better

Can you make your letter better?

Of course, you can. It's probably not as difficult as you might think. Some people get bogged down in the letter-writing process. It may be because they have a fear of writing, which could include the fear of misspelling a word or making a grammatical error. Plenty of the early learning process with the elementary teacher included corrections and red marks for making mistakes.

To make the process easier, use this simple form:

Letter Project:	
Purpose:	
Who Will Receive the Letter:	
Topic/Scope:	
Desired Action:	

This form is for your own use. Using a pen or pencil, write your answers freely:

Letter Project:	*Revitalize fading customers.*
Purpose:	*Turn inactive customers into active customers— increase total sales from these inactive customers from 0 to 15 percent or total quarterly sales goals.*
Who Will Receive the Sales/Pitch Letter:	*Letters will target past customers that are not ordering from us any longer. Any customer who has not placed an order within the past six months will receive the letter.*
Topic/Scope/ Important Points:	*1. Tell customer we miss their business* *2. Remind customer of our past relationship.* *3. Inform customer of new product lines added since last order.* *4. Make special offer to get customer back into active status.*
Desired Action:	*Turn inactive customers into active customers.*

This simple form and your answers can help you focus the purpose of your letter by identifying what it is that you want to accomplish. Breaking your writing job down by realizing what it is you want to accomplish can help you produce a better sales or pitch letter.

The next step is to write. Use a pen or pencil and a legal pad, or begin typing on a computer screen; whatever works for you. Don't worry about the format, spelling, penmanship, or typing. This is often called freewriting (some call it dumping). The idea is to get the stuff out of your head. Here is how your first attempt at the fade away letter might look:

> We miss you. We miss your business. You were a good
> customer in the past. We have an offer you need to consider.
> Come back to us now to get a discount of toner cartridges. Two
> more lines added. Send you a catalog. Whatever you need. New
> guarantee. Need you to place order asap so you can get special
> 2-for-1 deal ending this month.

Of course, you will need to go back and revise your letter. Step 1 is to get your thoughts organized and down on paper or on the computer. The next part—often the hardest for many people—is the revision and editing process. Here are the steps:

1. Start writing to a person you know (or think you know), rather than an anonymous customer.

2. Write an opening sentence: "It's been too long since you've ordered Atlas Toner Cartridges from us."

3. Tell your past customer why: "You nearly dropped off our radar screen, which means you would have missed our special 2-for-1 sale."

4. Add some urgency: "But you have to order now, because our sale is going to end on the last day of this month. That's only nine days away."

5. Offer more information: "Since you last purchased toner cartridges from us, we have added two more product lines. We now have more than 1,000 printing products than we had six months ago. And our satisfaction guarantee has been expanded; you can return anything you bought from us for up to one year—for full credit—with no questions asked."

6. Close your letter: "I'd like to see that you get our new catalog, and our discounted price list, and also get you back on to our active customer list. I will do whatever it takes to have you agree that we are your vendor of choice when it comes to office supplies. Let's save you and your company money now by ordering a year's supply of toner cartridges—but only paying for six month's worth."

Your finished letter will look like this:

> It's been too long since you've ordered Atlas Toner Cartridges from us.
>
> You nearly dropped off our radar screen, which means you would have missed our special 2-for-1 sale. However, you have to order now, because our sale is going to end on the last day of this month. That's only nine days away.
>
> Since you last purchased toner cartridges from us, we have added two more product lines. We now have over 1,000 more printing products than we had six months ago. And our satisfaction guarantee has been expanded. You can return anything you bought from us for up to one year—for full credit—with no questions asked.
>
> I'd like to see that you get our new catalog, our discounted price list, and get you back on to our active customer list. I will do whatever it takes to have you agree that we are your vendor of choice when it comes to office supplies. Let's save you and your company money now by ordering a year's supply of toner cartridges—but only paying for six months worth. If you haven't ordered within the next three days, I'll try to contact you by phone so you don't miss this special sale, which is available only to our past customers.

This may not be a perfect letter, but it is worthy of testing. If it works, you can send it to other customers similar to the friend you tried it out on. You may need to change the items and descriptions, but your effort of building a letter is not nearly as difficult if you first determine the purpose and scope, free write the letter, and then refine it. Don't worry about making errors in the first or second attempt. At first, you just want your ideas to formulate, and then to get them down on paper. There is plenty of time to refine and edit, making your letters better. Check your letter against your original intent. Ask yourself:

- Does my letter focus on the recipient?
- Is the scope of the letter clear and meaningful?
- How is my letter organized?
- How effective is my closing?
- Is my letter grammatically correct?
- How have I used the sentences to construct paragraphs?
- Do I have a good mix of sentence length?
- Are there two or more sentences to a paragraph?
- Do all of the sentences of a paragraph complement each other and build on the same thought?
- Have I used language effectively?

Don't Forget Your Goals

Your sales and pitch letters must:

> ▷ Catch the recipient's attention.

> ▷ Appeal to the letter reader's current desires, needs, or wants.

> ▷ Clarify your product or service.

> ▷ Stimulate the reader to take action now.

These four items must be included in every letter. Sometimes creating them is easy, while other times you may have had a hard time trying to find the right word to convey your message.

Keep in mind the audience of your letter. Your approach to a 19- to 23-year- old college student is likely to different from a 62- to 66-year-old facing retirement. How does your letter fit the goals you have identified for the letter?

Edit and Edit Some More

Editing is a process. Don't be afraid to set your letter aside, and review it later. Look for ways to rewrite anything that is muddy or unclear. Keep in mind the common rule of keeping your writing simple.

Don't be afraid to cut words, especially if it makes your writing clearer. If you have long sentences, find ways to change them into two sentences. Strike out all unnecessary sentences and words. Use direct, unambiguous statements. Strip out all empty hype words such as "incredible," "basically," "amazing," and "best ever." Cut all clichés from your letters.

Get Input From Others

If there are others in your office who are available, get their opinion of your letter. Additional input never hurts; what might seem clear to you could generate a very different meaning to someone else. Listen carefully to constructive criticism and make appropriate change.

Read It Backwards

One trick that works is to read a piece of writing from the bottom to the top. Read the last sentence first. Then the next to the last sentence, and so on. Each sentence should make sense, and be able to stand alone. If you detect any problems, make the necessary changes.

Look for Problems

Avoid being long-winded in your letters. When you have something to say, say it, and move on. If you don't follow this simple advice, your correspondence will become boring.

Be unique in your letters, and be cautious about being like all other letters. Don't just offer a generalized statement such as "we really are the best" or "we really want your business."

 Maintain a file of sales letters you receive. Some will stand out more than others. Consider why some work, and why others are less effective.

Check Your Sentences

As you revise your writing, check your sentences for:

- Length—no more than 30 words per sentence (and remember 25 words is better than 30, and 20 is better than 25). Use long sentence sparingly.

- Thought—try to keep each sentence to one thought, and two thoughts at most.

- Varied—change your sentence structure. Keeping sentences the same becomes boring. For example: The toner is black. The toner is improved. The toner is less expensive. The toner is guaranteed. The toner is available now. The toner is on sale.

Don't try to include too much information in your letter. Keep your message and the information simple, straightforward, and uncomplicated. Use brochures and other sales documents to provide the extensive details, and tie together the brochures with your newsletter. Don't try to include everything that's in your brochures into the body of your letter.

Use Layout to Enhance Your Letter

Simple design elements can make your correspondence easier to read and comprehend, along with improving the appearance. Some the things you can do include:

- Adding bulleted lists.

- Adding numbering.

- Including text elements, such as capitalization, italics, underscoring, and punctuation.

Don't Overdo It!

Consider this simple example:

> I'd like to see that you get our NEW CATALOG, our **DISCOUNTED PRICE LIST**, and *get you back* onto our <u>active customer list</u>!!! *I will do* whatever it takes to have you agree that we are your **VENDOR OF CHOICE** when it comes to OFFICE SUPPLIES!!! Let's **save you** AND **your company money** now <u>by ordering a year's supply</u> of **TONER CARTRIDGES**, but only paying for six months worth!!! **If you haven't ordered within the next three days**, I'LL CALL YOU so you **DON'T MISS OUT** on this **special sale**—AVAILABLE ONLY TO OUR PAST CUSTOMERS!!!!!!!

Now review the same text, with only two words embellished:

> I'd like to see that you get our new catalog, our discounted price list, and get you back onto our active customer list. I will do whatever it takes to have you agree that we are your vendor of choice when it comes to office supplies. Let's save you and your company money now by ordering a year's supply of toner cartridges—but only paying for six months worth. If you haven't ordered within the next three days, I'll call you so you don't miss out on this **SPECIAL SALE**—available only to our past customers.

The point is simple: Overusing design elements can lead to clutter, amateur or unprofessional images, or images that should be avoided. Use capitalization, underlines, italics, and bold-face type, but use them sparingly for maximum design impact.

Use Proper Business Titles

Titles in business have their own hierarchy. For most companies, associations, and corporations, the hierarchy moves from the chairperson of the board down to the line managers and supervisors. There are many possible titles, and each organization have developed their own titles and usage. A list of the common titles is as follows:

- ▷ Chairperson of the Board.
- ▷ President.
- ▷ C.E.O.
- ▷ President and Chief Executive Officer.

- ▷ Executive Vice President.

- ▷ Associate Vice President.

- ▷ Vice President.

- ▷ Officer of the Comptroller.

- ▷ Officer of the Corporate Secretary.

- ▷ Officer of the Treasurer.

- ▷ Manager.

- ▷ Director.

- ▷ Supervisor.

- ▷ Superintendent.

- ▷ Sales Manager.

Your correspondence should always be addressed to a specific person. The order of each line remains the same:

Person's name

Title

Company

Street Address

City, State, Postal Zip Code

Always include the person's title in the inside address. The title may follow the individual's name or be listed underneath the name, such as:

Mary C. Charles

Director of Home Sales

Franklin County Homes

302 Lincoln Drive

Fictionaltown, FL 32809

Dear Ms. Charles:

or

Mary C. Charles, Director of Home Sales

Franklin County Homes

302 Lincoln Drive

Fictionaltown, FL 32809

Dear Ms. Charles:

Do not use the title as part of the salutation:

Mary C. Charles, Director of Home Sales

Franklin County Homes

302 Lincoln Drive

Fictionaltown, FL 32809

Dear Ms. Charles, Director of Home Sales:

 Tip Find out the recipient's title before you write the letter. Knowing the correct title tells the recipient that you have taken to the time to learn who they are.

If you cannot possibly learn the name of the person at the company or organization that holds the position, you can write to the position in this manner:

Director of Home Sales

Franklin County Homes

302 Lincoln Drive

Fictionaltown, FL 32809

Dear Director of Home Sales:

Are You Ready for a Large Response?

Before sending out mass amounts of sales letters, calculate the highest possible response you or your organization can actually handle. Make certain that you are in a position to handle the increased business from your clients and prospects. Some sales letter campaigns will fizzle, but others can be extremely successful. Can you handle an unusually high response? Don't create the perfect pitch and then be unable to fulfill all the orders that come in?

Testing Your Letters

There are three words of advice for anyone that is planning a sales or pitch letter campaign: Test. Test. Test.

When you're planning a large mailing, send out a few different versions of your sales letter to small groups, and then see what pulls by measuring the results.

For example, if you have created a longer letter, test it by shortening it. Some have reported that eight-page letters, which have been reduced to four-page letters, sell just as well, yet by going to one sheet of folded paper, the cost of production was cut nearly in half. If you test, you can determine if you really do need a longer document to get the same (or better) results.

Some letters and sales campaigns just work better than others do. Instead of spending your entire budget on one campaign, test first to make sure your letters will work on a larger sample.

Mail Merge Overload

Resist overloading your prospects and customers with never-ending mail-merge-produced documents (mail merge is the insertion of names and addresses from a database into the body of the correspondence). Your computer and software can easily produce innumerable electronic documents. Your best sales letters—those that will get the most results—are practical and individualized as much as possible. Don't fall into the trap of sending letters just for the sake of mailing, and only because the work involved is made easier with today's technology. Avoid mailing just to mail something to your clients, prospects, and customers. Make sure there is both a clear message and purpose of sending your sales and pitch letters.

Consider the Long Term

As you work on your sales and pitch letters, don't get caught up in pushing services or products. High-pressure sales should not be the goal. You should want to develop a long-term relationship with your customers. Don't pressure your client or customer into one discounted sale. Use your sales letter to investigate whether you can solve customer problems. Always try to build a long-term relationship that will last with your customer.

Phrases That Work

Some phrases seem to work well in sales and pitch letters. Use them to help you get started writing your letters. Here are some phrases you can use:

1. "As soon as your order arrives here on my desk, I will immediately..."
2. "While looking over our records, I observed that..."
3. "If you're like me, you have probably..."
4. "You are cordially invited to..."
5. "I look forward to talking with you about this in more detail when we meet next week."

6. "If you have any questions or would like to discuss this further, please feel free to give me a call."

7. "And there's no risk to you. If you are not completely satisfied, just return your _____ and I'll send you a full refund, no questions asked."

8. "Let me list __ reasons why you should..."

9. "Did you know that...?"

10. "The deadline is..."

Editing

When writing your sales and pitch letters, a part of the final process is editing your correspondence. Editing is the final preparation of the content before it is presented to your prospects, clients, and customers.

Think of editing as the refinement—the last chance to evaluate your prose with a critical eye. Your intention is not criticism, but, rather, the review and correction of errors, grammar, spelling, and syntax. The editing process also includes the final review of the intent of the correspondence.

There are many different ways and techniques to edit. Most of the time, you will be your own editor. While there is nothing wrong with serving as your own editor, it often is best to have someone else, whenever possible, to review and edit your sales and pitch letter. When completing your own editing, don't rush the process. Moreover, *never* skip the editing.

Some people confuse editing with proofreading. Editing occurs *before* proofreading (often called proofing). After editing, the sales or pitch letter is prepared for distribution. After typesetting, layout, and printing, the letter is proofed (to make sure it looks good, makes sense, and contains no errors). Following proofing, the letter is then sent to the client, customer, or prospect.

5 Easy Steps to Improve Your Editing

1. Let your letter stand or rest. In other words, after writing the letter, don't edit it immediately. Set it aside, and look at it later. By waiting, perhaps a day or so, you can give your letter a fresh look.

2. Read each sentence, but start from the bottom, and work backward. It may not make sense, but cover up your letter with a blank piece of paper, exposing only the last sentence. Read it first. Then reveal the second to last sentence, and read it. Reviewing in a backward order often allows you to detect problems.

3. Read your letter aloud. Reading the correspondence and speaking the words often alerts you of any problems.

4. If you doubt anything, make edits. If a sentence doesn't seem right, or if you question spelling or word usage, don't be lazy. Edit, make changes, or rewrite. If it doesn't seem right, it probably isn't.

5. Develop your own checklist, based on your writing tendencies. Some people naturally write longer sentences. Others may have the inclination to overuse specific words, such as put, got, or perusal. Add these kinds of annoying or weak writing techniques to a list, and then specifically look for these problems in the sales and pitch letters.

Proofing the Letters

After you have edited and prepared your correspondence, it is time for the final proofing. You should not find errors, but it still your goal to spot them. You do not want to send out anything that is not 100-percent perfect. Misspellings, grammatical mistakes, and formatting appearance are the reason for proofing.

If you are preparing the letters by using automatic mail merge functions, it is critical that you proof the letters before sending. Mail merge can often produce errors during the integration process. There could be errors in the database or the letter, which can turn off the reader of your sales or pitch letter.

Depending on the merge software, your correspondence may include an error code. For example, the code may look something like this:

Mr. <!ERROR: Merge Field not found!>, you can trust our company to deliver quality service.

Obviously, you would not want to send this letter. However, many people sloppily dispense this somewhat hasty, unproofed correspondence.

5 Tips When Using Mail Merge Software

1. Take the time to learn the merge feature of your software. Taking a few minutes to master the procedures can save lots of time and frustration later.

2. Test your merge repeatedly to make sure that you have set up the fields in your correspondence, and that they match your database fields.

3. Watch your text formats. Some programs preserve the format of the data when it is merged into the primary document. Your letter might be written in Times New Roman, but the data is stored in Ariel font. Each data field would be different in the final merged document.

4. Check your spacing! Merging creates sloppy appearances when spacing is not carefully created. For example, you might set up a document like this:

    <firstname><lastname>
    <address>
    <city>, <state><zip>

    and when merged with your records from your database file, the result would look like this:

    GeorgeWashington
    1600 Pennsylvania Avenue
    Washington, D.C. 20000

    With proper spacing with the fields:

    <firstname><lastname>
    <address>
    <city>, <state><zip>

    The results would be:

    George Washington
    1600 Pennsylvania Avenue
    Washington, D.C. 20000

5. When using the merge software to send e-mail messages, make sure you can prevent the automatic merging and sending without a final review. You may need to modify your e-mail software to prevent sending until you authorize it. This extra step can prevent the mailing of correspondence that contains embarrassing merge errors.

Work Your Database

Tap your customer list for information about a particular customer's sales history and preferences. Send specialized sales letters whenever it is appropriate. For example, if a customer has not bought anything in six months, send a friendly "we miss you" letter, include a special offer specific to that customer, based on the customer's past purchases.

PART III
Sample Sales and Pitch Letters

Direct Selling Letters

As a business, you are selling a service or product, as well as your image. The sample letters in this chapter intend to sell you, your company, your products, and your services to prospects and clients. These letters intend to initiate a sale, including:

    ▷ Announcing a special offer.

    ▷ Announcing a new service.

    ▷ Announcing a new product.

    ▷ General announcements.

Use these letters as a general template or pattern for your own direct selling letters.

Keep these thoughts in mind:

    ▷ Direct selling letters are used by salespeople to commence the sales process. The purpose is not to make a sale in the letter, but rather to start the process. For example, imagine trying to sell a $150,000,000-million dollar jet in a short business letter.

    ▷ The letter is a mere sales tool. It is just one part of the entire process.

    ▷ Direct selling letters are often more creative than other kinds of business letters.

    ▷ Review the earlier chapters for help in creating and writing the different parts of your direct sales letters.

Announcing a Special Offer

[Company Letterhead]
[Company Name]
[Company Address]
[Company City, State, Zip]
[Company Phone/Fax/Website/E-mail]

[Date]

[First Name] [Last Name]
[Title]
[Company]
[Address]
[City], [State] [Zip]

Dear [Salutation]:

You might like to know that we have just expanded our 5-for-4 promotion to include thousands of items in our Home and Garden Store. Now, you can mix and match kitchen gadgets and appliances, towels and sheets, pet supplies, and more. We now offer more than 50,000 items.

How does it work? Just order five items, and we'll give you the lowest priced item for free when we invoice you.

Sincerely,

[Your Name]
[Your Title]

P.S. You can save $10, $100, or $1,000—it's up to you. But place your order today—our 5-for-4 promotion ends next week.

[Company Letterhead]
[Company Name]
[Company Address]
[Company City, State, Zip]
[Company Phone/Fax/Website/E-mail]

[Date]

[First Name] [Last Name]
[Title]
[Company]
[Address]
[City], [State] [Zip]

START PACKING NOW!

Dear [Salutation]:

Plan to get away now!

From now through [date], we are slashing our fares from [your city] to destinations around the country. Here are just a few examples of the roundtrip fares we're now offering:

▶ [city: fare]

▶ [city: fare]

▶ [city: fare]

And that's not all! If there's a city you want to visit this [season], there's probably a special fare we're offering!

At these amazing rates, seats are quite limited, and some certain restrictions do apply. (See [attachment/enclosure] for details.) Call our Reservations Desk—or visit our Website at [*www.website.com*]—for more details.

And don't forget, to start packing!

Sincerely,

[Your Name]
[Your Title]

ENCLOSURE

[Company Letterhead]
[Company Name]
[Company Address]
[Company City, State, Zip]
[Company Phone/Fax/Website/E-mail]

[Date]

[First Name] [Last Name]
[Title]
[Company]
[Address]
[City], [State] [Zip]

Dear [Salutation]:

The proof is in!

For years, we've been telling our customers that our [product] is the only one that has the [feature] to give you the results you need! Now we can prove it!

An independent survey proved that we are rated number one in reliability, and preferred 3 to 1 over [our closest competitor]. [Our product] really delivers what you want, and at an affordable price.

But you don't need to take our word for it; try it for yourself—absolutely FREE.

That's right, if you act now, you can take advantage of our special introductory offer and try [product] absolutely FREE for one month. All you have to do is call our toll-free number at (800) 555-5555, and we'll you send you [product] to try for 30 days at no charge. If you don't agree that our [product] is the best, pay us nothing. Just return [product] to us at our expense. If you decide to keep [product], you can finance it throughout the next 12 months, interest free.

Don't wait. This is a limited offer. Pick up the phone and call us now!

Sincerely,

[Your Name]
[Your Title]

P.S. Yes, try it FREE! No obligation, and no questions asked if you decide to return it.

[Company Letterhead]
[Company Name]
[Company Address]
[Company City, State, Zip]
[Company Phone/Fax/Website/E-mail]

[Date]

[First Name] [Last Name]
[Title]
[Company]
[Address]
[City], [State] [Zip]

Dear [Salutation]:

I DARE YOU to take our [product] challenge!

Our [product type] is so far ahead of the competition, most others haven't come close to catching up with our innovations. However, you can! [Product name] is not for people interested in doing business the same old way. It's for people like you: people that want to save time and make more money each day.

[Product] is available now. Improve your production by 20 percent during the next month, and you'll pay for the [product] within 90 days. Trying to find a better investment is impossible.

I dare you to take action. Here is an exclusive offer just for you: order from our Website by [date/time] and take 15 percent off your order!

Sincerely,

[Your Name]
[Your Title]

[Company Letterhead]
[Company Name]
[Company Address]
[Company City, State, Zip]
[Company Phone/Fax/Website/E-mail]

[Date]

[First Name] [Last Name]
[Title]
[Company]
[Address]
[City], [State] [Zip]

Dear [Salutation]:

If you could design the PERFECT lawn-care service, what would you ask for?

* Low monthly fees.

* Quality service, guaranteed.

* Dependable weekly service.

* Weed and pest control options.

* No contract.

Guess what? You're in luck! [Company] has already designed this perfect law care service for you!

AND FOR LIMITED TIME, YOU CAN GET YOUR
FIRST WEEK OF SERVICE FREE! JUST ORDER
BY [DATE] TO QUALIFY!

After your FREE initial week, you'll only pay $25.95 a month for everything you could want in a dependable lawn-care service.

Call (800) 555-5555 for more details, or check out our Website at [www.company.com]. You've got nothing to lose and everything to gain by switching to [company]'s complete lawn care service. Try it, and you'll agree there's nothing like [company] for GREAT, dependable service!

Sincerely,

[Your Name]
[Your Title]

[Company Letterhead]
[Company Name]
[Company Address]
[Company City, State, Zip]
[Company Phone/Fax/Website/E-mail]

[Date]

[First Name] [Last Name]
[Title]
[Company]
[Address]
[City], [State] [Zip]

Dear [Salutation]:

We sure did not plan to make purchasing a new [product] confusing. But with our showroom filled with a wide array of new models, we might have created a problem. There are so many new features, so many selections, and so many improvements, anyone could be baffled.

I'll help you. Let's arrange a time for you to visit our showroom at [location]. I'll personally walk you through the showroom, show you all the new items and features, and answer any of your questions, with no obligation, of course.

You will be amazed at our selection. I'll also have a special gift for you, just for stopping in and saying hello. It's best to make an appointment so I can give you my undivided attention. Call me at 555-5555 to arrange a time convenient to both of our schedules.

Sincerely,

[Your Name]
[Your Title]

[Company Letterhead]
[Company Name]
[Company Address]
[Company City, State, Zip]
[Company Phone/Fax/Website/E-mail]

[Date]

[First Name] [Last Name]
[Title]
[Company]
[Address]
[City], [State] [Zip]

Dear [Salutation]:

We seldom stick our necks out for someone else. But [product] is so unique and trustworthy, we just cannot remain silent.

In as few words as possible, [product] is just great! It is:

- Easy to use.
- Dependable.
- Reliable.
- Convenient.
- Cost Effective.
- Durable.

We think you should try [product] now. To help you make the decision to use [product], we're offering a 2-for-1 sale. Buy one package of [product], and get a second free. Of course, our 100-percent-satisfaction guarantee is available—but no one has returned any [product] yet. In fact, our customers have been ordering additional packages almost immediately after they try [product]. You should try it, too. But hurry, as our 2-for-1 sale ends on the 21st of this month.

Sincerely,

[Your Name]
[Your Title]

[Company Letterhead]
[Company Name]
[Company Address]
[Company City, State, Zip]
[Company Phone/Fax/Website/E-mail]

[Date]

[First Name] [Last Name]
[Title]
[Company]
[Address]
[City], [State] [Zip]

Dear [Salutation]:

Last week was our biggest sale ever! I marked down all the furniture, bedding, and floor covering at [Company Name]. It was the lowest price in three years—and many items have not been marked this low in more than five years!

The results were amazing. Our customers recognized the great values, and we sold more furniture that week than any other week in our history.

I decided to do it again—next week only—but there is a catch. To get the discounted price, you must bring this letter to the store; no letter, no discount.

Plan now to save at [Company Name]. Bring this letter to the store to get your special, discounted price—available only to our past customers.

Sincerely,

[Your Name]
[Your Title]

[Company Letterhead]
[Company Name]
[Company Address]
[Company City, State, Zip]
[Company Phone/Fax/Website/E-mail]

[Date]

[First Name] [Last Name]
[Title]
[Company]
[Address]
[City], [State] [Zip]

Dear [Salutation]:

It's spring and new products are arriving. That's especially true at [Company Name].

I am writing to invite you to our special spring sale. We've added more than 250 new items in our store, and everything is discounted 20 percent (or more) during our sale. You will never find a better time to save on [items].

In the past, our special spring sale has always been an event our valued customers enjoy. For the best selection, and to avoid any disappointment, mark your calendar now. It's [date]—one day only to save on all things new at [Company Name].

See you at the spring sale!

Sincerely,

[Your Name]
[Your Title]

[Company Letterhead]
[Company Name]
[Company Address]
[Company City, State, Zip]
[Company Phone/Fax/Website/E-mail]

[Date]

[First Name] [Last Name]
[Title]
[Company]
[Address]
[City], [State] [Zip]

Dear [Salutation]:

Stop. Look. Listen.

That's what you should do this week at [Company]. *Stop* at [address]. *Look* at the new line of [Product]. *Listen* to reasons why you should be using [Company] as your complete source of [Product].

Why should you stop, look, and listen now? Because we have a special offer for you: buy $1,000 or more in supplies, and take 90 days to pay. Why wait? Keep your cash and pay within the next three months. Can you really afford not to stop in and look at our complete line of [Product]?

Sincerely,

[Your Name]
[Your Title]

[Company Letterhead]
[Company Name]
[Company Address]
[Company City, State, Zip]
[Company Phone/Fax/Website/E-mail]

[Date]

[First Name] [Last Name]
[Title]
[Company]
[Address]
[City], [State] [Zip]

Dear [Salutation]:

Here is your free pass to our new tanning center, [city's] newest facility. It features the latest tanning beds, designed to help you look your best without damaging your skin.

Your free pass grants you unlimited use of all facilities at no cost for two weeks. We want you to evaluate our new state-of-the-art facility. Experience how great you feel and look after regular tanning sessions at [company].

When your complimentary pass expires, you will be able to extend your membership at our regular low rates. Or for the best possible price, become a member during your first visit and get a full year's membership for half price.

Stop by tomorrow and use your free pass. We are easy to find, right beside [local landmark].

Sincerely,

[Your Name]
[Your Title]

ENCLOSURE

[Company Letterhead]
[Company Name]
[Company Address]
[Company City, State, Zip]
[Company Phone/Fax/Website/E-mail]

[Date]

[First Name] [Last Name]
[Title]
[Company]
[Address]
[City], [State] [Zip]

Dear [Salutation]:

Using [product] is fast and simple! Other similar products are complicated, troublesome, and require extensive maintenance. But not [product]—you can learn to use it in fewer than 15 minutes. A new menu system makes [product] as easy to use as your TV remote.

You can get started immediately with a new [product], because our crews can complete the installation in one day. Your staff will be trained and making money for you within 24-hours. And if you act now, we'll give you a start up package of supplies—that's more than a $500 value.

Call me today at 555-5555 if you have any questions. We can also discuss an installation in your office.

Sincerely,

[Your Name]
[Your Title]

[Company Letterhead]
[Company Name]
[Company Address]
[Company City, State, Zip]
[Company Phone/Fax/Website/E-mail]

[Date]

[First Name] [Last Name]
[Title]
[Company]
[Address]
[City], [State] [Zip]

IF YOU CALL US, A LIVE PERSON WILL ANSWER OUR PHONE.

Dear [Salutation]:

In today's world, many companies think the speed of business means they don't have to provide their customers with the personal touch. We feel the exact opposite. We don't use voice mail. We still answer the phone.

We believe that each of our customers deserves personalized service. You, too, can experience this by calling (800) 555-5555. Any one of our customer service representatives will listen and make sure you get the right part to fit your needs quickly. And our service doesn't stop when the product is delivered; our support hotline is open seven days a week from 7 a.m. to 10 p.m. Get your questions answered any time.

Call us now at (800) 555-5555 to get the parts and the service you need. Mention this code: **AD89** to receive a 20-percent discount on your first order.

Sincerely,

[Your Name]
[Your Title]

P.S. Hurry! This 20 percent off expires June 30.

[Company Letterhead]
[Company Name]
[Company Address]
[Company City, State, Zip]
[Company Phone/Fax/Website/E-mail]

[Date]

[First Name] [Last Name]
[Title]
[Company]
[Address]
[City], [State] [Zip]

Dear [Salutation]:

We know you'd rather be golfing than shredding documents. But those darn regulations and lawsuits make shredding a part of your duties.

Let us help. Our new high-speed shredder makes it a breeze to destroy your most sensitive documents. Our professional staff will remove the documents from your office, shred them in our mobile unit, and either return the destroyed documents for your disposal, or take them away for you.

Don't waste your valuable time on shredding. Act now to get your first 200 pounds of documents shredded free! You can take advantage of this limited-time offer until the end of the month. Don't waste another minute shredding documents.

Sincerely,

[Your Name]
[Your Title]

[Company Letterhead]
[Company Name]
[Company Address]
[Company City, State, Zip]
[Company Phone/Fax/Website/E-mail]

[Date]

[First Name] [Last Name]
[Title]
[Company]
[Address]
[City], [State] [Zip]

Get Distinctive Now.

Dear [Salutation]:

There are many marketing materials out there vying for your customers' attention. What you need is a stamp of distinction.

That's where we can help. We give your brochure, flyer, envelopes, and letterheads a distinctive look with customized die cutting, hot embossing, and foil stamping. We can custom design any type of printing you need, from business cards to presentation folders, from envelopes to letterheads.

Let us take 25 percent of our first printing job for you. We'll make sure your printed materials stand out from the other with your own distinctive designs. For more information, call (800) 555-5555.

Sincerely,

[Your Name]
[Your Title]

[Company Letterhead]
[Company Name]
[Company Address]
[Company City, State, Zip]
[Company Phone/Fax/Website/E-mail]

[Date]

[First Name] [Last Name]
[Title]
[Company]
[Address]
[City], [State] [Zip]

Dear [Salutation]:

We will start our summer sales campaign on May 1.

In the past, this campaign has enabled us to offer our customers a wide selection of products at competitive prices. It is an outstanding way to attract new customers and build traffic for your business.

I have enclosed our latest catalog for your review.

All orders have to be in by June 15 to receive a 15-percent discount off our regular low prices.

As always, it will be my pleasure working with you. Thank for your continued business.

Sincerely,

[Your Name]
[Your Title]

Announcing a New Service

[Company Letterhead]
[Company Name]
[Company Address]
[Company City, State, Zip]
[Company Phone/Fax/Website/E-mail]

[Date]

[First Name] [Last Name]
[Title]
[Company]
[Address]
[City], [State] [Zip]

Dear [Salutation]:

It's been a long time since we've spoken, so I thought I'd update you on a few things we're doing that would be of interest to you.

We now offer a new promotions service, which allows you to provide sales incentives to your customers. We'll fill orders for you after your customers submit coupons.

We also have a new Website-based rebate system. This is working well for wholesale promotions. I've enclosed a brochure about both of these new services for your review.

I'll call you in a few days to answer any questions, and to see if we can put our creative team to work on developing new promotions for you.

Sincerely,

[Your Name]
[Your Title]

[Company Letterhead]
[Company Name]
[Company Address]
[Company City, State, Zip]
[Company Phone/Fax/Website/E-mail]

[Date]

[First Name] [Last Name]
[Title]
[Company]
[Address]
[City], [State] [Zip]

Dear [Salutation]:

I understand that you have started marketing your new business.

I respect your decision, but as a marketing professional, I do want to provide you with some facts, should your initial attempt prove frustrating:

> ▶ We represent a tradition of sales success. We have created successful marketing and advertising campaigns for hundreds of new businesses throughout the years.

> ▶ Increased advertising helps generate business for you. However, where can you get the biggest bang for the buck? What works, and what won't? Our experience—more than 30 years—tells us where to begin a campaign for a business such as yours.

> ▶ We work with businesses of all sizes—and specialize in new enterprises.

You might be thinking you can't afford us. Actually, you can't afford not to work with us. We guarantee results—in writing. Please permit me the opportunity to speak with you personally.

I look forward to your phone call.

Sincerely,

[Your Name]
[Your Title]

P.S. You are assured of a 25-percent increase in business in the first week— guaranteed in writing—or you don't pay us anything!

[Company Letterhead]
[Company Name]
[Company Address]
[Company City, State, Zip]
[Company Phone/Fax/Website/E-mail]

[Date]

[First Name] [Last Name]
[Title]
[Company]
[Address]
[City], [State] [Zip]

Dear [Salutation]:

It is time to get EXCITED! You won't believe the benefits for you and your company when you use our insurance billing service.

Our new service is so great, customers tell us they've never seen anything as FAST, EFFECTIVE, and INEXPENSIVE. Here are actual customer comments:

- "I have never experienced anything this effective—even with insurance billing services that cost twice as much."

- "I used another company before, but [Company] is the first one that really worked."

- "I signed up one day, and they started invoicing the next day! Our cash flow improved almost overnight!"

You must try our new insurance billing service for yourself to believe it.

Call (800) 555-555 TODAY, and sign up for your FREE 30-DAY TRIAL. That's right—we'll do your invoicing for the next 30 days—at no expense to you. Let us improve your cash flow—and get your collections up to where they should be.

Sincerely,

[Your Name]
[Your Title]

[Company Letterhead]
[Company Name]
[Company Address]
[Company City, State, Zip]
[Company Phone/Fax/Website/E-mail]

[Date]

[First Name] [Last Name]
[Title]
[Company]
[Address]
[City], [State] [Zip]

Dear [Salutation]:

Our firm recently received an extremely favorable review from the *Philadelphia Inquirer*, which we hope may be of some interest to you. In case you missed it, I have enclosed a copy with this letter.

Because our security service lends itself so well to your business, we would appreciate having an opportunity to speak with you, or one of your representatives, about how we can help you to cut down on unnecessary overhead expenditures.

I will call you next week to arrange a meeting with you.

Sincerely,

[Your Name]
[Title]

P.S. We just saved a company smaller than yours more than $50,000 with our fraud-detection audit.

ENCLOSURE

[Company Letterhead]
[Company Name]
[Company Address]
[Company City, State, Zip]
[Company Phone/Fax/Website/E-mail]

[Date]

[First Name] [Last Name]
[Title]
[Company]
[Address]
[City], [State] [Zip]

Dear [Salutation]:

I'd like to introduce you to [Company] and our new service: computer network maintenance. Think of us as your quiet partner; most of the time you won't even know we're there.

But in an emergency, you can count on us. We will respond to your staff within 60 minutes, or we will pay you $5 for each minute we don't return your call.

We understand your needs, and can give you the service you deserve! Let's keep your computer network working.

Call (800) 555-5555 now for a free, no-obligation briefing of our computer network maintenance service.

Sincerely,

[Your Name]
[Your Title]

[Company Letterhead]
[Company Name]
[Company Address]
[Company City, State, Zip]
[Company Phone/Fax/Website/E-mail]

[Date]

[First Name] [Last Name]
[Title]
[Company]
[Address]
[City], [State] [Zip]

Dear [Salutation]:

Congratulations on the recent purchase of your new home!

Once you unpack, you'll want to establish a new lawn on your property. We can help. Our new lawn-care service seeds and feeds your new lawn. You'll have the greenest grass in your neighborhood within weeks.

We also offer the seeds, fertilizers, and tools that you'll need, if you want to do it yourself.

You can get your lawn established for less than you think, too. For less than $1 a day, you can have a plush new yard. Let's get your yard green now—call me at (800) 555-5555.

Sincerely,

[Your Name]
[Your Title]

[Company Letterhead]
[Company Name]
[Company Address]
[Company City, State, Zip]
[Company Phone/Fax/Website/E-mail]

[Date]

[First Name] [Last Name]
[Title]
[Company]
[Address]
[City], [State] [Zip]

Dear [Salutation]:

Need to ship 1,000 boxes to your customers? Want to send a package to Europe? Need some (or many) color copies? Boxes? Stamps? Shipping supplies?

There's an innovative way to take care of all your mailing and shipping needs.

We specialize in packing items of any size—from large household furnishings to precious jewelry.

Most shipments can be delivered by the next business day, whether you need it shipped across town or across the country.

Our office and main shipping depot are at 987 South West Street, one block south of the bus depot. We maintain a supply of big and little boxes, tape, bubble wrap, mailers, envelopes, and much more to make your packing and shipping fast and easy. Bring your packages to us, or give us a call and we'll pick up your shipment at your business.

Our hours are 8 a.m. to 8 p.m., seven days a week. Let us handle your shipping needs—we'll make it so much easier on you and your staff.

Sincerely,

[Your Name]
[Your Title]

[Company Letterhead]
[Company Name]
[Company Address]
[Company City, State, Zip]
[Company Phone/Fax/Website/E-mail]

[Date]

[First Name] [Last Name]
[Title]
[Company]
[Address]
[City], [State] [Zip]

Dear [Salutation]:

I am happy to introduce our new staffing service to you.

When you need a temporary manufacturing worker, call us at (800) 555-5555. We'll supply you with the work force you need to get the job done.

Sincerely,

[Your Name]
[Your Title]

[Company Letterhead]
[Company Name]
[Company Address]
[Company City, State, Zip]
[Company Phone/Fax/Website/E-mail]

[Date]

[First Name] [Last Name]
[Title]
[Company]
[Address]
[City], [State] [Zip]

Dear [Salutation]:

Some businesses may want to wait for our Close-on-the-15th Service to establish a long record of accomplishment in the marketplace. Nevertheless, business leaders with prudence know that sitting on the fence in this fast-paced world can be deadly to a company's market position.

[Company] is the innovative way to get your books closed in the middle of the month. By doing so, you can see quick results including:

- Improved cash flow.
- Avoiding the end-of-the-month crunch.
- Better work flow with your office staff.

Call us today at (800) 555-5555 to find out how our new Close-on-the-15th Service can help your business.

Sincerely,

[Your Name]
[Your Title]

[Company Letterhead]
[Company Name]
[Company Address]
[Company City, State, Zip]
[Company Phone/Fax/Website/E-mail]

[Date]

[First Name] [Last Name]
[Title]
[Company]
[Address]
[City], [State] [Zip]

New Service Can Protect Your Business

Dear [Salutation]:

Last month, the local news reported the fire that destroyed the Old Mill. There was more than $2 million dollars of damage. The fire destroyed three businesses. Now the fire marshal determined the cause: faulty wiring.

One business was back to serving its customers within 24 hours. That's because they wisely chose [Company name] to provide off-site back-up service. Jim Grove of Grove's Payroll Service says, "[Company name] saved us. With more than 500 clients, and more than 2,500 people depending on us to produce their paychecks, we needed a comprehensive back-up service. [Company name] had us back in business before the fire department had left the scene. I cannot say enough good things about you. We were able to stay in business and function like nothing happened—even though we lost our entire office."

Isn't it time for you to consider what [Company name] can do for you, too? No one knows when the next disaster might happen. Don't take chances. Depend on [Company name] to protect your important data.

Let's sit down and review your data disaster recovery plan. It's something no business should be without—and we will provide you with a free, no-obligation plan.

Sincerely,

[Your Name]
[Your Title]

[Company Letterhead]
[Company Name]
[Company Address]
[Company City, State, Zip]
[Company Phone/Fax/Website/E-mail]

[Date]

[First Name] [Last Name]
[Title]
[Company]
[Address]
[City], [State] [Zip]

CALL ME NOW BEFORE A CRISIS DEVELOPS!

Dear [Salutation]:

The stamina of any successful businesses is its ability to consistently produce accurate documents with a professional image. Your reputation—and eventually your bottom line—depends on the appearance and fast turnaround time of your correspondence, documents, and reports. When a business suddenly finds itself short staffed or facing a temporary work overload, the outcome is too often a disastrous disruption in workflow and customer service.

Developing a working relationship with a dependable document-processing service, such as mine, is an effective way to avoid any staffing crisis. I can offer you the business experience and computer skills you need to complete a special project, meet an important deadline, or help you through a transitional period (such as when a member of your office support staff is on maternity leave or vacation).

Why wait until you have a crisis? Let's set up a brief meeting now at your office to discuss working to keep your business running seamlessly during staff shortages or work overloads.

Sincerely,

[Your Name]
[Title]

P.S. I can help make your employees more valuable to you by automating their work, and improving their computer skills. This investment will pay for itself repeatedly.

Announcing a New Product

[Company Letterhead]
[Company Name]
[Company Address]
[Company City, State, Zip]
[Company Phone/Fax/Website/E-mail]

[Date]

[First Name] [Last Name]
[Title]
[Company]
[Address]
[City], [State] [Zip]

Dear [Salutation]:

Yes, it's completely true. You can replace your old, worn-out drill press and only pay $517 out of your pocket—but only if you are one of the first six people to respond to this letter.

Let me explain.

Last month, our small company took a big gamble and signed up for a Dynamic KL-100 Drill Press promotion offered directly by the manufacturer. To get in on the special promotion, we agreed to accept 24 KL-100 drill presses—nearly $55,000. (And for a small company like us, that's a lot of money to be tied up in one product.)

Eighteen were sold—so there are six left. And my boss says sell them now.

My problem is your opportunity to save money: To move these last six drill presses, I've opted to do something bold, and a little enterprising.

First, you should know the manufacturer's promotion of these drill presses ends July 31st. Any unsold inventory I still have could be sold to another dealer at wholesale. Instead of doing that, I would rather sell you the drill press at a wholesale price and gain your goodwill.

The regular price for a Dynamic KL-100 Drill Press is $6,000, but during this promotion, they are on sale for $5,285 (and that is a pretty good deal anyway). But until August 15th (I've extended the offer two weeks), you can buy one of our last six KL-100 drill presses for just $3,285. That's a savings of $2,715.00!

I promised you could get a KL-100 for only $517 and here's how....

By buying a KL-100, you can qualify for a 50-percent tax credit under section 44 of the Americans with Disabilities Act. All because the KL-100 adjusts up and down to allow disabled and handicapped workers. You can also take the amount of the KL-100 and deduct it off your taxes using Section 179. (That is if you haven't spent more than $20,000 on capital equipment this year.)

That's not all, here are a few more incentives for you to consider:

Page 2

We will give you a $3,000 trade-in for your old press (or you could donate it to a charity for another tax break). We're adding in an extra 2-year warranty ($1,000 value), plus we'll pick up your old drill press and deliver and setup the new KL-100—all at no cost for you!

And I have even better news for you....

With this special promotion, you can use our 90-day, same-as-cash program. Now you can pay in three easy installments with NO interest. Do the math—it turns out that a new KL-100 will only cost $517. How can your shop be without one?

You must respond before August 15th! First, I doubt if these drill presses will still be around until August 15th, because the first six shops that respond and place their orders will take them. This is a one-time only offer—it will never be repeated. When they're gone, this special offer expires.

But even if they are still here—which is unlikely at this bargain price—this offer must expire. That's because we will be shipping out the remaining KL-100s to other dealers in the country. We must make room in our warehouse for the fall inventory.

Here's what you should do now: Pick up your phone and call me at 717-7179. Reserve one of these last six KL-100's now.

If you're still undecided, call me. I'll be glad to answer any questions and fax more information to you. If you want to "test-drive" a KL-100, you can do that, too, here at our showroom. I'll be glad to arrange a hands-on, no-obligation demonstration.

Don't delay. If you do, you'll be giving up the ability of adding a new KL-100 drill press at this bargain price. When these six are gone, the next one we sell will be for $6,000.

I really hope you're one of the six lucky machine shops that decide to take advantage of this special opportunity.

Sincerely,

[Your Name]
[Title]

P.S. Hurry! This letter is being sent to 783 local shops. This offer is strictly and absolutely limited to the first six that respond.

[Company Letterhead]
[Company Name]
[Company Address]
[Company City, State, Zip]
[Company Phone/Fax/Website/E-mail]

[Date]

[First Name] [Last Name]
[Title]
[Company]
[Address]
[City], [State] [Zip]

THE BAD NEWS AND THE GOOD NEWS

Dear [Salutation]:

I've got some good news and some bad news for you.

The bad news is you probably paid too much for your last photocopier.

The good news is that it never has to happen again. In a recent survey, we found that our copiers are consistently priced lower than our competition. So why are you paying too much for the features you want most, such as networking, color reproduction, and auto-collating?

The next time you need a photocopier, stay on budget: remember the good news, and look to us for your needs.

Sincerely,

[Your Name]
[Your Title]

[Company Letterhead]
[Company Name]
[Company Address]
[Company City, State, Zip]
[Company Phone/Fax/Website/E-mail]

[Date]

[First Name] [Last Name]
[Title]
[Company]
[Address]
[City], [State] [Zip]

Dear [Salutation]:

This letter is worth $350 to you, so don't throw it away!

Stop by at our equipment showroom during the next five days, and I'll reduce the price of any new or pre-owned copier by $350! And that's with our already discounted prices! So, if you've been thinking about replacing that old copier of yours with a new, affordable digital copier that you'll be proud to use, call me today.

Your documents will sparkle. Color is now an affordable—and necessary—choice in today's competitive market.

Don't miss our special "Say Good-bye to Winter Sale." All prices have been slashed, and if you bring in this letter to me before April 1, I'll save you $350 more! It's that easy.

Call me today to set up an appointment.

Sincerely,

[Your Name]
[Your Title]

P.S. Did you know we offer a 120-day, same-as-cash program for all units under $5,000?

[Company Letterhead]
[Company Name]
[Company Address]
[Company City, State, Zip]
[Company Phone/Fax/Website/E-mail]

[Date]

[First Name] [Last Name]
[Title]
[Company]
[Address]
[City], [State] [Zip]

We proudly announce the birth of a bouncing new baby—our new lawn-care utility trailer.

Dear [Salutation]:

It'll grow on you!

It took us a while, but our new lawn-care utility trailer was designed, refined, manufactured, and safely delivered. It's our best design yet—with all the features our customers told us they wanted.

Our new trailer has a perfect lineage. It is born from the latest technology, and married to an innovative design. Together, we created a utility trailer that brings a new generation into the world of lawn-care specialists.

Come see our proud new addition today, or call me at (800) 555-5555, and I'll bring our new baby to you, so you can see all the features of our newest creation. And it's guaranteed not to eat you out of house and home.

Sincerely,

[Your Name]
[Your Title]

P.S. To celebrate this happy occasion, you can get a $500 rebate if you order your own baby within the next 45 days!

[Company Letterhead]
[Company Name]
[Company Address]
[Company City, State, Zip]
[Company Phone/Fax/Website/E-mail]

[Date]

[First Name] [Last Name]
[Title]
[Company]
[Address]
[City], [State] [Zip]

Dear [Salutation]:

It's time. Reward yourself now with new office furniture.

You've worked hard to achieve all of your success, and you've finally made it. Congratulations! Let's celebrate with a new XL-100.

You've probably had your eye on an upgraded executive desk system for some time. Now we make it easy for you to own one. They're on sale—20 percent off this month—and you can finance one with a 90-day, same-as-cash purchase. But this offer is only good for those in stock in our warehouse. With this sale, you need to act now.

The enclosed flyer describes all the benefits of owning the XL-100 system.

Order today! Call me at (800) 555-5555 now.

Sincerely,

[Your Name]
[Your Title]

[Company Letterhead]
[Company Name]
[Company Address]
[Company City, State, Zip]
[Company Phone/Fax/Website/E-mail]

[Date]

[First Name] [Last Name]
[Title]
[Company]
[Address]
[City], [State] [Zip]

Dear [Salutation]:

We're pleased to announce a new addition to our family of products. The new digital D200 printer is designed to save you time and money.

As a loyal customer, you know that we only carry quality products. We want our customers to be 100-percent satisfied with anything they purchase from us. We select products built to last—and to look great for years to come. The D200 is no different.

Come in today and get your D200 with a sorter at no extra charge.

Sincerely,

[Your Name]
[Your Title]

[Company Letterhead]
[Company Name]
[Company Address]
[Company City, State, Zip]
[Company Phone/Fax/Website/E-mail]

[Date]

[First Name] [Last Name]
[Title]
[Company]
[Address]
[City], [State] [Zip]

Dear [Salutation]:

We are quite pleased to announce a new addition to our family of products. The new oak roll-top is designed with the refined tastes of the sophisticated consumer in mind.

As a loyal customer, you know that we only use the finest materials and craftsmanship for our products. They're built to last—and to look great for years to come. The classic country oak roll-top desk is no different.

Come in today and get your desk with a matching oak chair—at no extra charge. But hurry: this offer ends in two weeks.

Sincerely,

[Your Name]
[Your Title]

P.S. You can still get the desk and a chair after the two weeks is up, but it will cost $499 more.

[Company Letterhead]
[Company Name]
[Company Address]
[Company City, State, Zip]
[Company Phone/Fax/Website/E-mail]

[Date]

[First Name] [Last Name]
[Title]
[Company]
[Address]
[City], [State] [Zip]

STOP LOSING SLEEP!

Dear [Salutation]:

Do you lay awake at night wondering how to solve your problems with fulfilling your product orders?

Well worry no more! The solution is here at last!

We can end those sleepless nights with our new K8 model. Our machine can triple your current production, and cost less to operate. We can also show you how to reduce scrap. Most customers find they pay for the K8 within the year just with their scrap reduction alone.

Call me now and let's get your order for a K8 processed today. There is no reason for you lose another night's sleep over your production worries.

Sincerely,

[Your Name]
[Your Title]

[Company Letterhead]
[Company Name]
[Company Address]
[Company City, State, Zip]
[Company Phone/Fax/Website/E-mail]

[Date]

[First Name] [Last Name]
[Title]
[Company]
[Address]
[City], [State] [Zip]

Dear [Salutation]:

Most American companies ignore the Asian market. That's because they have no idea how eager Asian people are for products such as yours.

We help companies make sales throughout Asia. One of our clients, who produces dental instruments, sold more than 25,000 units in just six months. We set up distribution for them, and we can do the same for you. Will you give me a few minutes to explain how you can build new sales and markets by taking advantage of the opportunities in the Asian market?

I'll call to schedule an appointment.

Sincerely,

[Your Name]
[Your Title]

[Company Letterhead]
[Company Name]
[Company Address]
[Company City, State, Zip]
[Company Phone/Fax/Website/E-mail]

[Date]

[First Name] [Last Name]
[Title]
[Company]
[Address]
[City], [State] [Zip]

ACT NOW!

Dear [Salutation]:

Special introductory offer! Limited time only!

Purchase a new D200 within the next 10 days, and you'll get the special D218-x free.

Get all the features you've wanted—and a great accessory to match—FREE!

But you must act now.

Call me at (800) 555-5555 today.

Sincerely,

[Your Name]
[Your Title]

[Company Letterhead]
[Company Name]
[Company Address]
[Company City, State, Zip]
[Company Phone/Fax/Website/E-mail]

[Date]

[First Name] [Last Name]
[Title]
[Company]
[Address]
[City], [State] [Zip]

REDUCE INJURIES NOW

Dear [Salutation]:

With the proper equipment, you can reduce injuries in your warehouse and increase productivity by as much as 40 percent.

Many of our customers find that the right equipment can pay for itself with three to six months of reduced worker's compensation insurance costs.

We offer free consulting to assist you when choosing the equipment that will allow your materials to be handled at the safest working height for your equipment operator.

It makes good business sense to reduce injuries to your personnel. Let's start the process now. I'll call you within the next few days to discuss the process with you.

Sincerely,

[Your Name]
[Your Title]

[Company Letterhead]
[Company Name]
[Company Address]
[Company City, State, Zip]
[Company Phone/Fax/Website/E-mail]

[Date]

[First Name] [Last Name]
[Title]
[Company]
[Address]
[City], [State] [Zip]

Dear [Salutation]:

It's fresh! It's new! Now it can be yours!

We are proud to introduce our new D200. It's smaller, faster, and stylish. And best of all, it's energy-efficient, costing less to operate.

You can use your new D200 to produce your customer's customized orders. It will cost less to produce those banners and signs. Isn't that exactly what you're looking for in a banner printer?

Act now! Return the enclosed card today! Your new D200 can be in your shop within a week!

Sincerely,

[Your Name]
[Your Title]

ENCLOSURE

[Company Letterhead]
[Company Name]
[Company Address]
[Company City, State, Zip]
[Company Phone/Fax/Website/E-mail]

[Date]

[First Name] [Last Name]
[Title]
[Company]
[Address]
[City], [State] [Zip]

Dear [Salutation]:

We've just acquired the XYZ Company. That means their entire product line of clamps and related tools have been added to our catalog.

This expands our product line to more than 10,000 items. Our new catalog will be sent to you as soon as they are available. In the meantime, if you need any clamps, call me.

I am pleased to offer a special introductory discount to you. All the XYZ Company's products are on sale now with a 20-percent discount. The introductory sale ends June 15, so order today!

Sincerely,

[Your Name]
[Your Title]

[Company Letterhead]
[Company Name]
[Company Address]
[Company City, State, Zip]
[Company Phone/Fax/Website/E-mail]

[Date]

[First Name] [Last Name]
[Title]
[Company]
[Address]
[City], [State] [Zip]

Dear [Salutation]:

Using the D200 is fast and simple! Other similar products are complicated, troublesome, and require extensive maintenance. But not the D200—you can learn to use it in less than 15 minutes. A new menu system makes the D200 as easy to use as your TV remote.

You can get started immediately with a new D200—our crews can complete the installation in one day. Your staff will be trained and making money for you within 24 hours. And if you act now, we'll give you a start-up package of supplies—that's worth more than $500.

Call me today at 555-5555 with any questions you might have. We can also discuss an installation in your office.

Sincerely,

[Your Name]
[Your Title]

[Company Letterhead]
[Company Name]
[Company Address]
[Company City, State, Zip]
[Company Phone/Fax/Website/E-mail]

[Date]

[First Name] [Last Name]
[Title]
[Company]
[Address]
[City], [State] [Zip]

Dear [Salutation]:

Now is the time to try the D200. When you do, you can expect:

- Better colors.

- Brighter results.

- Bigger orders.

One customer told me that since they switched to the D200, "our results have been unbelievable. Our sales are up more than 300 percent. Our downtime has been reduced to nil. Simply, the D200 has been the best investment we have ever made. Thanks for bringing this to our attention. You have helped us make a lot of money these past 90 days."

Shouldn't you be making a lot of money, too? Isn't it time for you to test the D200?

May I schedule an appointment with you next week? What day would be the most convenient for you?

Sincerely,

[Your Name]
[Your Title]

[Company Letterhead]
[Company Name]
[Company Address]
[Company City, State, Zip]
[Company Phone/Fax/Website/E-mail]

[Date]

[First Name] [Last Name]
[Title]
[Company]
[Address]
[City], [State] [Zip]

Dear [Salutation]:

Our Secret Summer Sale is about to get underway, and we want to remind you of the substantial savings we offer during this annual event.

For two weeks only, every photography accessory will be marked down by a minimum of 15 percent. Every book on photography will be marked down 25 percent. All flash equipment will be marked down 20 percent. Need I say more?

This incredible sale begins on June 1 and will end at 9 p.m. sharp on June 14. We know you won't want to miss this one!

Sincerely,

[Your Name]
[Title]

P.S. Need a new telephoto lens? We have more than 10 different models available at 20 percent off our regular price. Call me now—I don't have many in stock.

[Company Letterhead]
[Company Name]
[Company Address]
[Company City, State, Zip]
[Company Phone/Fax/Website/E-mail]

[Date]

[First Name] [Last Name]
[Title]
[Company]
[Address]
[City], [State] [Zip]

Dear [Salutation]:

I am sending the attached advertisement artwork for the Independence Day holiday for your consideration. The format and design can be used to promote this occasion as a direct mail piece, in-house handout, or as a newspaper advertisement. The illustrated ads that we enclosed were designed for a standard 8-column newspaper.

We hope that you find this no-obligation offer as exciting as we do, and will consider it for the holiday. You can depend on our high quality of offset printing to assure your complete satisfaction with the finished product.

When you decide to place your order, please contact me at 555-5555. If I can be of help to you in any additional way, please don't hesitate to call.

Sincerely,

[Your Name]
[Title]

P.S. I've enclosed a certificate, so your firm can save $250 off your next printing order!

ENCLOSURE

General Announcements

[Company Letterhead]
[Company Name]
[Company Address]
[Company City, State, Zip]
[Company Phone/Fax/Website/E-mail]

[Date]

[First Name] [Last Name]
[Title]
[Company]
[Address]
[City], [State] [Zip]

LOOKING FOR A BETTER HEALTHCARE INSURER?
ONE WITH A HIGHLY SUCCESSFUL TRACK RECORD?

Dear [Salutation]:

If you are, please take a look at me....

- Sixteen years of healthcare insurance experience...providing solutions for small one-person businesses to corporations with more than 30,000 employees.

- A proven record of accomplishment in getting the best rates for employers...in the last five years, I achieved a 42 percent increase in savings for my clients—when everyone else was paying more—LOTS MORE—for their employee healthcare products.

- Innovative and creative...developed and managed DIABETIC LINE, the first professionally answered, Q&A national telephone service...it has answered more than 100,000 calls at an average rate of 250 calls per day.

- Ideas that work...with documented results to show that health care benefits can cost less—if your programs are properly managed.

Page 2

▶ An accomplished diplomat...effective with executive, administrative, and medical personnel. Together, we can get the job done!

▶ An established reputation...known for being a motivated achiever of even the most difficult parts of setting up new medical benefits for employees. (I specialize in working with labor unions. After seeing my programs, your union will also want the coverage I offer, which will save you thousands of dollars each month.)

I'm ready to help you spend less and provide better care for all of your employees. Let's talk next week.

Sincerely,

[Your Name]
[Your Title]

[Company Letterhead]
[Company Name]
[Company Address]
[Company City, State, Zip]
[Company Phone/Fax/Website/E-mail]

[Date]

[First Name] [Last Name]
[Title]
[Company]
[Address]
[City], [State] [Zip]

Dear [Salutation]:

A great deal of care goes into choosing the most appropriate banker for your needs. I believe we meet our customers' needs through a combination of the "old-fashioned ways" of banking, personal contact at each one of our branches, and employing the latest technology. Our personal commitment is to you, our customer.

I hope you will investigate our small business services, and because some of the products we offer may seem confusing at first, I'd like to invite you to a "get to know each other" meeting at my office. The more I understand about your business and banking needs, the more I will be able to offer just what you need.

I have enclosed our latest financial statement for your review, with a descriptive brochure of the many services available to small businesses, such as yours. If I may, could I suggest we sit down together next week—just for a chat—so we can both get to know each other better? I think it could be beneficial to both of us.

Sincerely,

[Your Name]
[Your Title]

P.S. When we meet, be sure to ask me about our new small business program, which includes no fees and no minimum account balance requirements.

[Company Letterhead]
[Company Name]
[Company Address]
[Company City, State, Zip]
[Company Phone/Fax/Website/E-mail]

[Date]

[First Name] [Last Name]
[Title]
[Company]
[Address]
[City], [State] [Zip]

Dear [Salutation]:

Someone once said that words are cheap. That was decades ago. A poorly written letter to a business associate, potential customer, or dissatisfied user can be costly—and trigger a costly lawsuit.

Our publication, "How to Avoid Lawsuits Triggered by Bad Writing," offers solid advice on how to get the job done, and at the same time, prevent costly lawsuits. It's the same publication we use to deliver our employee training programs.

We are so confident that you will appreciate the advice in our publication that we are offering you the opportunity to inspect and read it for 10 days.

By returning the enclosed card, we will mail your copy of "How to Avoid Lawsuits Triggered by Bad Writing" to you immediately. It will give you a chance to assess if our employee training programs could help you avoid costly litigation.

Please fill out the card today.

Sincerely,

[Your Name]
[Your Title]

P.S. One nuisance lawsuit can cost thousands of dollars in legal expenses. Your staff can learn quickly how to avoid libel charges.

ENCLOSURE

[Company Letterhead]
[Company Name]
[Company Address]
[Company City, State, Zip]
[Company Phone/Fax/Website/E-mail]

[Date]

[First Name] [Last Name]
[Title]
[Company]
[Address]
[City], [State] [Zip]

Dear [Salutation]:

We know exactly what your lawn needs are! Our trained professionals will work to make your lawn greener and weed-free, so you can have more time to enjoy it.

Contact us today for a free lawn analysis at 555-5555 for all your lawn and landscape needs.

Sincerely,

[Your Name]
[Your Title]

[Company Letterhead]
[Company Name]
[Company Address]
[Company City, State, Zip]
[Company Phone/Fax/Website/E-mail]

[Date]

[First Name] [Last Name]
[Title]
[Company]
[Address]
[City], [State] [Zip]

Dear [Salutation]:

DID YOU KNOW?

The trained professionals at [Company] specialize in:

- Yard and field.

- Post hole digging.

- Brush hogging and field mowing.

- On-site lawn mowing, whether it is just while you are on vacation, or for an entire season.

Insured and dependable service. Call us now at 555-5555.

Sincerely,

[Your Name]
[Your Title]

[Company Letterhead]
[Company Name]
[Company Address]
[Company City, State, Zip]
[Company Phone/Fax/Website/E-mail]

[Date]

[First Name] [Last Name]
[Title]
[Company]
[Address]
[City], [State] [Zip]

Dear [Salutation]:

WE MOW FAST!

The speed and maneuverability of our lawn-care and mowing service will you allow you spend more time with your family in your yard. We take care of the work, so you can do the things you really want to do. Not only will we save you time and money, but the result will be a beautifully cut lawn.

You'll be the envy of your neighborhood!

Sincerely,

[Your Name]
[Your Title]

[Company Letterhead]
[Company Name]
[Company Address]
[Company City, State, Zip]
[Company Phone/Fax/Website/E-mail]

[Date]

[First Name] [Last Name]
[Title]
[Company]
[Address]
[City], [State] [Zip]

Dear [Salutation]:

TAKE THE SUMMER WEEKENDS OFF

Why waste your hard-earned weekends when you can let the experts at [Company] take the reins and make your lawn the greenest on the block? We are here to make your lawn-care experience both beneficial and pleasurable.

Call us now for a free estimate.

Sincerely,

[Your Name]
[Your Title]

P.S. Limited time offer: free spring fertilizer application to make your grass greener than ever! Call today and get scheduled! A $100 value—FREE!

[Company Letterhead]
[Company Name]
[Company Address]
[Company City, State, Zip]
[Company Phone/Fax/Website/E-mail]

[Date]

[First Name] [Last Name]
[Title]
[Company]
[Address]
[City], [State] [Zip]

Dear [Salutation]:

Don't have time to research your lawn-care needs? Let our experts give your lawn a free analysis! Our lawn-care system destroys weeds and kills pests!

Call us at 555-5555 to schedule a no-obligation appointment.

Sincerely,

[Your Name]
[Your Title]

[Company Letterhead]
[Company Name]
[Company Address]
[Company City, State, Zip]
[Company Phone/Fax/Website/E-mail]

[Date]

[First Name] [Last Name]
[Title]
[Company]
[Address]
[City], [State] [Zip]

GUARANTEED!

Dear [Salutation]:

We provide your lawn and home with these guarantees:

- You can say good-bye to those annoying brown spots.

- We use effective natural insecticides.

- We kill ants.

We do understand that every lawn has weeds and pests! It's 100-percent beneficial to act right away. For a limited time, we will give you a week's worth of lawn-care free! Call us today at 555-5555 for complete details of this limited offer.

Sincerely,

[Your Name]
[Your Title]

[Company Letterhead]
[Company Name]
[Company Address]
[Company City, State, Zip]
[Company Phone/Fax/Website/E-mail]

[Date]

[First Name] [Last Name]
[Title]
[Company]
[Address]
[City], [State] [Zip]

Welcome to the Greater [Area/Location]

Dear [Salutation]:

We offer:

- Mowing and edging.

- Leaf removal.

- Garden tilling.

- Shrubs and tree trimming.

- Gutters cleaned.

- Hauling of any kind.

- Residential and commercial insured.

- Free estimates.

- Satisfaction guaranteed.

I am enclosing a special 50-percent-off coupon for your first lawn-care application. It's a special gift to welcome you to the neighborhood.

Sincerely,

[Your Name]
[Your Title]

[Company Letterhead]
[Company Name]
[Company Address]
[Company City, State, Zip]
[Company Phone/Fax/Website/E-mail]

[Date]

[First Name] [Last Name]
[Title]
[Company]
[Address]
[City], [State] [Zip]

A $45 SPECIAL!

Dear [Salutation]:

We pride ourselves on our ability to make a lawn look its finest!

We use commercial grade mowers: a perfect cut is guaranteed. There is also the option of having the grass mulched, which we highly recommend, or if you prefer, collected.

We are a small company with roots in the community that we serve, so we understand the importance of a well-maintained lawn. Call us today to schedule your first cutting at 555-5555. And for you to get to know us, your first lawn-cutting is only $45.

Sincerely,

[Your Name]
[Your Title]

[Company Letterhead]
[Company Name]
[Company Address]
[Company City, State, Zip]
[Company Phone/Fax/Website/E-mail]

[Date]

[First Name] [Last Name]
[Title]
[Company]
[Address]
[City], [State] [Zip]

Dear [Salutation]:

A PERFECT FIT—GUARANTEED

Fitting and adjusting is available for clothes bought at [Company] in the [Location/Area].

Our tailoring and fashion consultants are here for you. This service is free of charge, and without obligation to buy. Book your appointment with the tailor/ fashion consultants by e-mail or telephone.

The altered garment can be collected after three to five working days.

Express services are available for some urgent and simple alterations, which include hemming of sleeves and pants. The garments can be collected on the same or the following day.

Call us at 555-5555 and ask for complete details and prices.

Sincerely,

[Your Name]
[Your Title]

[Company Letterhead]
[Company Name]
[Company Address]
[Company City, State, Zip]
[Company Phone/Fax/Website/E-mail]

[Date]

[First Name] [Last Name]
[Title]
[Company]
[Address]
[City], [State] [Zip]

OLD-FASHIONED SERVICE FOR YOUR FASHION

Dear [Salutation]:

[Company] is a distinctive old-school tailor shop dedicated to serving your needs. No job is too big or too small for us. Whether you need to adjust the length of your new jeans, or would like to design your own prom dress, we will be glad to help you.

[Company] has been tailoring for more than 30 years. While fashions change, a good fit, attention to detail, and listening to you—YOU, the customer— never goes out of style. That is why some of [Location] best clothiers in the state have employed [Company].

Stop by! Give us a call at 555-5555, or e-mail us at company@company.com— we're always happy to hear from you, and provide you with great service!

Sincerely,

[Your Name]
[Your Title]

[Company Letterhead]
[Company Name]
[Company Address]
[Company City, State, Zip]
[Company Phone/Fax/Website/E-mail]

[Date]

[First Name] [Last Name]
[Title]
[Company]
[Address]
[City], [State] [Zip]

Dear [Salutation]:

Do you suffer from intense toe pain due to bunions or hammertoes? Do you have corns and calluses on your feet from shoes that don't fit right? If so, you might need orthopedic shoes.

Many of the conditions described are due to one thing: poorly fitting and poorly designed shoes. Wearing an orthopedic shoe, can help reverse some of these symptoms and keep you moving in comfort.

If you have swollen, problem-prone feet, you need a good pair of orthopedic shoes. Fortunately, [Company]—the comfort and foot-health expert—has a wide selection of orthopedic shoes to fit your busy lifestyle.

Your feet are the foundation of your body, and wearing good shoes—such as an orthopedic shoe—can help you live an active, pain-free life. Stop by our store—open Monday through Saturday, 10 a.m. to 6 p.m.

Sincerely,

[Your Name]
[Your Title]

[Company Letterhead]
[Company Name]
[Company Address]
[Company City, State, Zip]
[Company Phone/Fax/Website/E-mail]

[Date]

[First Name] [Last Name]
[Title]
[Company]
[Address]
[City], [State] [Zip]

Dear [Salutation]:

[Company] is a family-owned business, and we strive to give your formal occasion the personalized attention you deserve and desire. We provide expert fitting, and we know you will be pleased with our caring attitude and friendly service. Your satisfaction is very important to us; from helping with the selection of the appropriate tuxedo, to the perfect fitting garments, we take the time to do it right.

We are the only full-service formal wear shop on the gorgeous [Location]. We have the largest in-store inventory of tuxedos and accessories in the area. If you need a tuxedo immediately, we will fit you on the spot. In addition, we offer the latest styles of tuxedos and accessories through our contact with major suppliers in the United States. If you have seen it in a magazine, online, or in a formal wear shop, we can get it for you.

We know how important this event is to you, and we would be honored to help you with your formal-wear needs. You will be glad you chose us; that's a promise!

Our tuxedos start at $89. Stop in and browse, or have a fitting done.

Sincerely,

[Your Name]
[Your Title]

[Company Letterhead]
[Company Name]
[Company Address]
[Company City, State, Zip]
[Company Phone/Fax/Website/E-mail]

[Date]

[First Name] [Last Name]
[Title]
[Company]
[Address]
[City], [State] [Zip]

Dear [Salutation]:

[Company] is committed to celebrating pregnancy through smart, wearable, and chic designs and products. We look forward to continued growth and the opportunity to dress growing bellies everywhere.

We provide you with such fashionable choices as:

- Dresses.
- Jeans.
- Active wear.
- Nursing/lingerie.
- Diaper bags.

We offer hip maternity clothes for moms to be! Stop in! We have three convenient locations. Or, call us at 555-5555.

Sincerely,

[Your Name]
[Your Title]

P.S. I have enclosed a special 20 percent off coupon for you!

ENCLOSURE

[Company Letterhead]
[Company Name]
[Company Address]
[Company City, State, Zip]
[Company Phone/Fax/Website/E-mail]

[Date]

[First Name] [Last Name]
[Title]
[Company]
[Address]
[City], [State] [Zip]

WE'VE JUST OPENED OUR NEW FACILITY!

Dear [Salutation]:

Our new, modern facility and state-of-the art equipment allow us to provide the most comfortable care possible, including:

- Same-day emergency care.

- Preferred provider for all major insurances.

- 0-percent interest financing.

- Special care for anxious patients.

Now offering evening hours—schedule your appointment by calling 555-5555.

Sincerely,

[Your Name]
[Your Title]

[Company Letterhead]
[Company Name]
[Company Address]
[Company City, State, Zip]
[Company Phone/Fax/Website/E-mail]

[Date]

[First Name] [Last Name]
[Title]
[Company]
[Address]
[City], [State] [Zip]

FREE EXAM FOR NEW PATIENTS

Dear [Salutation]:

Dr. Johnson is offering a free dental examination for new patients. Schedule your exam now. We are located near City Hall, on Fourth Street. Our new facility offers easy parking, and we have evening hours, too.

There is no reason not to get your free examination. Don't put off your dental care.

Sincerely,

[Your Name]
[Your Title]

[Company Letterhead]
[Company Name]
[Company Address]
[Company City, State, Zip]
[Company Phone/Fax/Website/E-mail]

[Date]

[First Name] [Last Name]
[Title]
[Company]
[Address]
[City], [State] [Zip]

**Introducing the Revolutionary Dermabrasion Skin Care System—
The Exclusive Skin Peel System!**

Dear [Salutation]:

Your exclusive provider in the [Location] is only at [Company]. This breakthrough treatment combines noninvasive exfoliation with deep delivery of skin-specific solutions to improve and revitalize your skin. Schedule your FREE consultation now by calling us at 555-5555, and see how we can:

- give you fresher-looking skin.

- address your unique skin-care needs.

- use methods that are completely painless.

- recommend skin care supplements.

Sincerely,

[Your Name]
[Your Title]

[Company Letterhead]
[Company Name]
[Company Address]
[Company City, State, Zip]
[Company Phone/Fax/Website/E-mail]

[Date]

[First Name] [Last Name]
[Title]
[Company]
[Address]
[City], [State] [Zip]

Offering Fine European Clothing and Accessories

Dear [Salutation]:

Spring Jackets at 25 percent off—Bermuda Shorts 50 percent off—Sale Ends April 20.

- ◆ Gift certificates—any amount.
- ◆ Custom jewelry—starting at $10.
- ◆ Loads of leather wallets starting at $15.

Stop in today or visit us on the Web at [*www.company.com.*]

Sincerely,

[Your Name]
[Your Title]

[Company Letterhead]
[Company Name]
[Company Address]
[Company City, State, Zip]
[Company Phone/Fax/Website/E-mail]

[Date]

[First Name] [Last Name]
[Title]
[Company]
[Address]
[City], [State] [Zip]

Dear [Salutation]:

If you are avoiding high-impact aerobics, pregnant, have an injury or physical restriction, or are a senior citizen, this is the idea program for you! Come to a free BOXERCISE class.

We offer three great convenient locations.

Sincerely,

[Your Name]
[Your Title]

P.S. I have enclosed a free pass for you. Use it anytime—we're open seven days a week!

ENCLOSURE

[Company Letterhead]
[Company Name]
[Company Address]
[Company City, State, Zip]
[Company Phone/Fax/Website/E-mail]

[Date]

[First Name] [Last Name]
[Title]
[Company]
[Address]
[City], [State] [Zip]

Tired of Paying High Repair Prices?

Dear [Salutation]:

We service: mufflers, tires, batteries, brakes, shocks, and struts in all makes and models.

Qualified, knowledgeable, and experienced auto technicians are ready to keep you on the road—stop by or schedule an appointment by calling 555-5555.

Sincerely,

[Your Name]
[Your Title]

P.S. Save 50 percent on your next oil change—see the enclosed coupon!

ENCLOSURE

[Company Letterhead]
[Company Name]
[Company Address]
[Company City, State, Zip]
[Company Phone/Fax/Website/E-mail]

[Date]

[First Name] [Last Name]
[Title]
[Company]
[Address]
[City], [State] [Zip]

Dear [Salutation]:

With our showroom filled with a wide array of new models, we might have created a problem. Anyone could be baffled at the new features, selections, and improvements. It may be hard to wrap your head around it.

We can help. Let's arrange a time for you to visit our showroom at [location], and I will personally show you all the new features, and answer any of your questions.

You will be amazed at our selection. It's best to make an appointment so I can give you my undivided attention. Call me at 555-5555 to arrange a time convenient to both of our schedules.

Sincerely,

[Your Name]
[Your Title]

[Company Letterhead]
[Company Name]
[Company Address]
[Company City, State, Zip]
[Company Phone/Fax/Website/E-mail]

[Date]

[First Name] [Last Name]
[Title]
[Company]
[Address]
[City], [State] [Zip]

Dear [Salutation]:

Here's the plain truth about starting your own dentistry practice, and one remarkable, but exclusive program, that works.

His name is Doctor Robert Franklin, DDS, and he has more than 20 years of marketing expertise honed razor sharp while building his own practice. Dr. Franklin has been studying the marketing of dentistry for years, and is deeply concerned about what is interested for practitioners.

Dr. Franklin is deeply concerned when he sees dentists, who honestly want to grow a practice, following a path of certain failure and destruction. If you've tried a dental marketing program and have still been unable to grow your practice, it's probably NOT YOUR FAULT. In fact, there are several reasons why this has happened to you. I promise, YOU CAN SUCCEED, but what we see in marketing dental services right now is of serious concern.

Right now, for an extremely limited time, Dr. Franklin is offering a copy of a special manifesto about dramatically and quickly growing your dental practice.

Get your copy now by calling (800) 555-5555.

Sincerely,

[Your Name]
[Your Title]

P.S. If you could increase your monthly billings by 30 percent, what would that do to your annual bottom line?

[Company Letterhead]
[Company Name]
[Company Address]
[Company City, State, Zip]
[Company Phone/Fax/Website/E-mail]

[Date]

[First Name] [Last Name]
[Title]
[Company]
[Address]
[City], [State] [Zip]

Dear [Salutation]:

I have spent some time researching your company, and I'm impressed. However, based on my independent research, which includes observing your products being sold at retail, I have identified three areas that would further improve your profitability.

1. I visited 30 stores that specialize in your product, but your product was available in only 12 of those stores. The other stores are good target accounts as they move great volume. As an independent sales representative, I am sure I can get your product on their shelves.

2. Only two of those 12 stores were using your display materials, and they were getting good results. We could take the experience of those two stores and educate every other retailer to the sales-generating potential of the displays.

3. One potential customer said she would be willing to stock all of your SKUs, but she can't find anyone to show her how to merchandise the line. Her concern might represent an opportunity for a regional promotion.

Page 2

Your competitor is test marketing a new product in select locations. I have some comments from those retailers and customers about how the new product is doing. We could discuss some ideas I have on what you might do in response to this new product.

I would like to make these ideas a reality for you. I can be reached at 555-5555. If I don't hear from you, I will follow up within the next few days.

Sincerely,

[Your Name]
[Title]

P.S. There is a new channel of distribution available to you that could add 7.5 percent volume to your top line. We should discuss this, too.

[Company Letterhead]
[Company Name]
[Company Address]
[Company City, State, Zip]
[Company Phone/Fax/Website/E-mail]

[Date]

[First Name] [Last Name]
[Title]
[Company]
[Address]
[City], [State] [Zip]

Dear [Salutation]:

I'd like to introduce myself, and my company, as a member of the Betty Jones Team. We're the top lenders in the area, and we have a long list of satisfied clients for whom we've obtained mortgages to buy their dream homes.

The Betty Jones Team chose us as one of their recommended lenders because of our consistency in delivering quality loans with competitive rates. We were notified that you have either already listed, or are thinking about, listing your property with Betty Jones; congratulations on your choice.

We were notified of your interest because, as team members, we'd like to play an integral part in marketing your home. Once your home is listed, we will offer every potential financing plan available to the buyer who purchases your property. And most importantly, every salesperson in Betty Jones' office will have that information to present to all their potential buyers.

We believe this is important because sometimes buyers may not be aware of all the different methods of financing your property. Did you know you could buy a property with as little as $500 down? It's true, and it's our job to make sure buyers understand these excellent financing opportunities.

Also, we'll be ready to aid you and the Betty Jones Team during the sale of your home by screening potential buyers, so you know they are qualified to get a mortgage before you accept their offer!

Page 2

In addition, if you're moving within Pennsylvania, you, too, can be preapproved under our mortgage program. This will save time, and eliminate any financing concerns while you shop for your new dream home. It will also make you a "same-as-cash buyer" in negotiations!

We're proud to be part of the Betty Jones Team. We want to make sure you're satisfied not only with your choice of real estate agent, but also with having a quality transaction delivered in record time, and with the highest net funds to you.

If you have any questions about financing, please feel free to call me, seven days a week, at 555-5555.

Sincerely,

[Your Name]
[Title]

P.S. We will preapprove your next home loan—at no cost to you.

[Company Letterhead]
[Company Name]
[Company Address]
[Company City, State, Zip]
[Company Phone/Fax/Website/E-mail]

[Date]

[First Name] [Last Name]
[Title]
[Company]
[Address]
[City], [State] [Zip]

Dear [Salutation]:

Your business experience has already proven the advantages of leasing needed equipment as opposed to purchasing it. Our extensive leasing experience gives us a real competitive edge in furnishing your firm with the maximum advantages, but a minimum of "red tape" and time delay in approving equipment leases.

We realize the importance in properly structuring an equipment lease. We know it must meet the specific needs and requirements of your company. That's why we have so many options, such as the $1 buyout program, or the 90-day no payment program. We also offer our customers the choice of rewriting existing leases.

Please contact me if you are even considering the future acquisition of more income producing equipment. I will be pleased to speak with you either in person or by telephone, whichever you desire.

Sincerely,

[Your Name]
[Title]

P.S. We approve 98.7 percent of our leases within three hours or less! What equipment do you need now?

Arranging Appointments

An important part of the sales cycle is setting up or arranging appointments. Sales and marketing personnel must often request meetings with prospects, clients, and customers. Of course, many people consider it just another sales call. Too often, they avoid calls and messages, or use technology to hide.

Although persistence can pay off, it is often worthwhile to send a sales or pitch letter to work your way into a meeting.

There are certain proven techniques that improve the chances of:

▷ your letter getting past (or being forwarded by) the secretary, administrative assistant, or personal assistant to your intended contact.

▷ your intended contact being interested in seeing you.

Use the five-second rule when composing your sales letters, opening statements, and headlines. You must grab the attention of the reader within five seconds. This is especially true when requesting an appointment. It is easier for the letter recipient to ignore your request than to say yes.

Remember: Your sales letter will be competing with other letters received that day, which were sent by sales representatives hoping to gain your target's attention. To get through the pile of other correspondences, your sales letter needs to be:

▷ good.

▷ professional.

▷ different.

▷ relevant.

You have about 15 to 20 words to catch the reader's attention. This why so many requests for appointments use headlines.

―――――

Headlines in Your Letters

When writing headlines, try not to use more than 10 words; shorter is always better. The headline is likely to be read first; always keep it short and succinct.

―――――

How do you treat unsolicited letters that you receive? Most of these letters go directly into your trash, and many are not even opened. A few seconds is all it takes for someone to decide whether to read a letter or discard it, and most likely, you do the same thing. A secretary or assistant will open your letter, and they, too, will decide in just a few seconds whether to read on or throw it away as "junk mail." If your intended contact gets the letter, it will only be a few second-decision whether to read on, or toss your letter.

Your goal may be a face-to-face meeting. In the sales process, you might want to aim first for a telephone appointment. It is during that qualifying discussion when you can explore the customer or prospects needs.

You can do a lot on the phone; your helpful questions can help you understand the current situation. As part of the sales process, you can then set a face-to-face meeting. Seeking only a telephone appointment as an initial aim often makes it easier to get the ball rolling, and your sales letter seriously considered. It also demonstrates that you have a professional appreciation of the value of your prospect's or client's time.

[Company Letterhead]
[Company Name]
[Company Address]
[Company City, State, Zip]
[Company Phone/Fax/Website/E-mail]

[Date]

[First Name] [Last Name]
[Title]
[Company]
[Address]
[City], [State] [Zip]

Easy Compliance With New Employment Laws

Dear [Salutation]:

When you next consider your arrangements for compliance with the new employment laws passed by the legislature, I would welcome the opportunity to explain your duties, responsibilities, and requirements to you.

Our clients have found compliance to be easier than they first heard, and they actually reduce their tax burden by following the often-confusing regulations associated with the new laws. In fact, most of our clients are reducing their tax burden by 10 percent when working with us.

I will telephone you soon to agree on a future contact time that suits your schedule.

Sincerely,

[Your Name]
[Your Title]

[Company Letterhead]
[Company Name]
[Company Address]
[Company City, State, Zip]
[Company Phone/Fax/Website/E-mail]

[Date]

[First Name] [Last Name]
[Title]
[Company]
[Address]
[City], [State] [Zip]

Local Businesses Overpaying Their State Taxes

Dear [Salutation]:

Did you pay too much money into the state government's tax coffers last year? More than 88 percent of local businesses do—don't be one of them!

The reason? The latest tax law offering new deductions was poorly understood. Learn how to save money under the new law by becoming our client.

Let me show you how you can act now to save on taxes later. My service is low cost, especially when you consider how much money you'll save by using it! Throughout the past decade, I've worked with numerous small businesses to help them better understand their tax situations under changing tax laws. I'd like to put my experience to work for you.

Shouldn't you take steps now, before the April-15th crunch, to get all the deductions you are entitled for?

I'll call you next week to set up a convenient time to meet. To thank you for talking with me, this first meeting is, of course, free. I look forward to helping you save money on your taxes.

Sincerely,

[Your Name]
[Your Title]

[Company Letterhead]
[Company Name]
[Company Address]
[Company City, State, Zip]
[Company Phone/Fax/Website/E-mail]

[Date]

[First Name] [Last Name]
[Title]
[Company]
[Address]
[City], [State] [Zip]

Dear [Salutation]:

I've tried to reach you by phone, and I have left messages, but I still really need to speak with you. I know you are busy, so here's the reason I have been trying reach you:

You need to speak to me about [service]. I can save you more than 30 percent of what your company is now spending. Imagine—a 30-percent reduction in your costs—how would that affect your budget?

[Client] switched to our [service] last December, and has already saved more than $10,000 during the first three months of this year.

We need to talk. I need 20 minutes of your time to explain our [service]. You can save your company thousands of dollars each year. Call me at 555-5555 and let's set a time for a quick meeting in your office.

Sincerely,

[Your Name]
[Your Title]

[Company Letterhead]
[Company Name]
[Company Address]
[Company City, State, Zip]
[Company Phone/Fax/Website/E-mail]

[Date]

[First Name] [Last Name]
[Title]
[Company]
[Address]
[City], [State] [Zip]

Dear [Salutation]:

I realize that your time is valuable. I will be brief and to the point.

Your business is facing a critical deadline. You must switch to state-approved air scrubbing by July 1, or lose your license. It's a matter of your company's survival.

That's where my product comes in.

Businesses similar to yours across the country are now using our BD300 to comply with the state mandate. They are giving it rave reviews. It is easy to use, and it provides exactly what they need. And using it gives executives like you peace of mind.

Surely, it'd be worth 15 minutes of your time to learn more about this outstanding product. I will call you next week to arrange a convenient time to meet.

Sincerely,

[Your Name]
[Your Title]

[Company Letterhead]
[Company Name]
[Company Address]
[Company City, State, Zip]
[Company Phone/Fax/Website/E-mail]

[Date]

[First Name] [Last Name]
[Title]
[Company]
[Address]
[City], [State] [Zip]

Dear [Salutation]:

I will be in town on April 3, and would like to meet with you at your office to discuss shipping supplies that you may need in the second half of the year.

I have enclosed our latest catalog. Please take special note of the highlighted items. They are special values or new products that you will want to take advantage of now.

I will contact you later this week to schedule an appointment on April 3. If you need to get in touch with me, call me at (800) 555-5555.

I look forward to speaking with you. Thank you for your consideration.

Sincerely,

[Your Name]
[Your Title]

ENCLOSURE

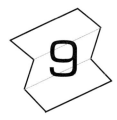

Follow-Up Letters

As you develop a relationship with a prospect or customer, keeping in touch is part of the marketing and sales cycle. Creating letters that maintain the relationship are generally easy to write, because of the relationship.

Rather than contacting someone you do not know, the follow-up letter is constructed to someone that you do know, or that knows of you or your organization. Often, the follow-up letter is a little less formal, or perhaps more conversational, in tone.

Follow-Up to a Telephone Conversation

[Company Letterhead]
[Company Name]
[Company Address]
[Company City, State, Zip]
[Company Phone/Fax/Website/E-mail]

[Date]

[First Name] [Last Name]
[Title]
[Company]
[Address]
[City], [State] [Zip]

Dear [Salutation]:

Thank you for calling us to discuss your current need for cleaning supplies.

As I promised, I am enclosing our most recent price list for your review.

If you need any additional information, please call me. It was a pleasure speaking with you.

Sincerely,

[Your Name]
[Your Title]

ENCLOSURE

[Company Letterhead]
[Company Name]
[Company Address]
[Company City, State, Zip]
[Company Phone/Fax/Website/E-mail]

[Date]

[First Name] [Last Name]
[Title]
[Company]
[Address]
[City], [State] [Zip]

Dear [Salutation]:

Thank you for calling [Company]. It was my pleasure to speak to you.

Your business is extremely important to me. Tell me what you need from us to change your status from a sale prospect to a satisfied customer. Whatever it is, we'll do it for you.

And if you are not totally satisfied, I'll make sure you are. You will be glad you became our customer; I personally guarantee that.

Thanks again for calling.

Sincerely,

[Your Name]
[Your Title]

[Company Letterhead]
[Company Name]
[Company Address]
[Company City, State, Zip]
[Company Phone/Fax/Website/E-mail]

[Date]

[First Name] [Last Name]
[Title]
[Company]
[Address]
[City], [State] [Zip]

SAVE $250—IF YOU ORDER THIS WEEK

Dear [Salutation]:

Last week when you called, we talked about the special discount being offered on the D200 system. This discount is only available once a year, and this year's offer expires at the end of this week.

If you're interested in the D200 system we talked about, call me and I'll reserve one for you. You will save $250, which is more than a 15-percent savings just by ordering your D200 this week.

Please remember, the price goes up next week, so call me today.

Sincerely,

[Your Name]
[Your Title]

[Company Letterhead]
[Company Name]
[Company Address]
[Company City, State, Zip]
[Company Phone/Fax/Website/E-mail]

[Date]

[First Name] [Last Name]
[Title]
[Company]
[Address]
[City], [State] [Zip]

Dear [Salutation]:

Thank you for discussing your current equipment needs with me.

As I mentioned, your company qualifies for our 120-day, same-as-cash program. You can make four payments throughout the 120 days. This makes it easier to get the equipment you need today, and pay for it later.

I'll call you next week to see if you are ready to purchase a D200 sorter. Of course, you can call me anytime to order, or discuss what your equipment needs are. We're ready to be of service to you, and become your vendor of choice.

Thanks again for calling us.

Sincerely,

[Your Name]
[Your Title]

[Company Letterhead]
[Company Name]
[Company Address]
[Company City, State, Zip]
[Company Phone/Fax/Website/E-mail]

[Date]

[First Name] [Last Name]
[Title]
[Company]
[Address]
[City], [State] [Zip]

Dear [Salutation]:

Since talking to you on the phone, I've completed the research we discussed, and I am enclosing the information you requested about the D200.

I have highlighted the compatibility issues that concerned you. As you will see, the D200 will work with your current equipment. But to make certain there are no problems, I will once again extend my offer to install a D200 in your office for your staff's use for the next two weeks. If you decide that the D200 does not save both time and money, we'll uninstall it. You can return it—no questions asked, and of course, no charge for the trial period. (By the way, I've never had a customer return a D200!)

Would you like to schedule a trial test this month?

Sincerely,

[Your Name]
[Your Title]

ENCLOSURE

Follow-Up to an Inquiry

[Company Letterhead]
[Company Name]
[Company Address]
[Company City, State, Zip]
[Company Phone/Fax/Website/E-mail]

[Date]

[First Name] [Last Name]
[Title]
[Company]
[Address]
[City], [State] [Zip]

Dear [Salutation]:

Thank you for your request for more information on our food quality pumps.

We have been distributing pumps since 1987, and we have more than 4,000 units in operation throughout the tri-state area.

We have an excellent reputation for quality, reliability, and service. All our products are designed, engineered, and manufactured in the United States.

I am enclosing a catalog that describes our complete line of food products.

Please contact me for more sales information, questions, or application assistance. It would be my pleasure to be of service to you.

Thank you once again for your interest our products.

Sincerely,

[Your Name]
[Your Title]

ENCLOSURE

[Company Letterhead]
[Company Name]
[Company Address]
[Company City, State, Zip]
[Company Phone/Fax/Website/E-mail]

[Date]

[First Name] [Last Name]
[Title]
[Company]
[Address]
[City], [State] [Zip]

Dear [Salutation]:

On July 1, I sent you a catalog sheet describing our newest product. Did you receive my correspondence? As you'll recall, you had requested information about the G405 fluid pump.

I will be happy to answer any questions you may have, and explain the unique features of our high-volume pumps.

You are a valued client and friend. If there is anything that I can do to help you make a decision, please call me at (800) 555-5555.

Sincerely,

[Your Name]
[Your Title]

[Company Letterhead]
[Company Name]
[Company Address]
[Company City, State, Zip]
[Company Phone/Fax/Website/E-mail]

[Date]

[First Name] [Last Name]
[Title]
[Company]
[Address]
[City], [State] [Zip]

Dear [Salutation]:

This is just a note to introduce myself, and to let you know of our interest in the 2010 meeting plans of your association.

Our facility contains 12 meeting rooms, which can be configured in numerous ways. We're located in the heart of Philadelphia, only 15 minutes from the airport or train station. There are more than two dozen four-star restaurants within four blocks of our location, offering all types of cuisine. We are adjacent to the largest on-site exhibition hall.

I have enclosed a brochure explaining our complete function space dimensions and capacities.

I will call your office next week to answer any questions you may have about our facilities, and to discuss how we may be of service to you. Thank you once again for contacting us.

Sincerely,

[Your Name]
[Your Title]

ENCLOSURE

[Company Letterhead]
[Company Name]
[Company Address]
[Company City, State, Zip]
[Company Phone/Fax/Website/E-mail]

[Date]

[First Name] [Last Name]
[Title]
[Company]
[Address]
[City], [State] [Zip]

Dear [Salutation]:

Thank you for visiting our booth at the Business Expo last week. I hope you enjoyed our demonstrations, and that you helped yourself to the free materials we had on display.

Since the Expo ended, we have been busy—but never too busy for our valued friends and customers. I want you to know that you can call me with any questions you might have at any time.

I am also enclosing a new product brochure that just became available on Tuesday. Check out the new mulcher, which can be mounted on a truck or trailer. We think this is one of the most exciting developments to come along in recent years.

Please let me know whether you would like additional copies of this brochure or any of the materials that were handed out at the convention. Please remember that I am only a phone call away if you have any questions.

Thank you once again for visiting our booth. It was a pleasure meeting you.

Sincerely,

[Your Name]
[Your Title]

ENCLOSURE

[Company Letterhead]
[Company Name]
[Company Address]
[Company City, State, Zip]
[Company Phone/Fax/Website/E-mail]

[Date]

[First Name] [Last Name]
[Title]
[Company]
[Address]
[City], [State] [Zip]

Dear [Salutation]:

I understand that a new D200 has been installed in your office. You chose right by purchasing a [product] from [company]. As you may remember from our discussions, the D200 has the lowest repair rate in the industry.

At the same time, the D200 is a machine, and, similar to all machines, they do occasionally break down. But you won't have to worry about lost productivity—call our service department and we'll have a technician in your office within four hours. And if your D200 cannot be quickly repaired, you'll get a free loaner.

We don't think business ends when we deliver a product, but rather it just begins. You are now our most valued asset: a customer, and we want you to be very satisfied.

Thank you for choosing us.

Sincerely,

[Your Name]
[Your Title]

[Company Letterhead]
[Company Name]
[Company Address]
[Company City, State, Zip]
[Company Phone/Fax/Website/E-mail]

[Date]

[First Name] [Last Name]
[Title]
[Company]
[Address]
[City], [State] [Zip]

Dear [Salutation]:

Thank you for choosing us as your payroll service.

I am going to call you several times throughout the next few weeks to make sure the transition from your former payroll service to us is going smoothly.

However, please contact me if you have any problems or concerns whatsoever. If any problems develop, I will immediately contact the division manager and get your issue resolved without any delay.

Thanks for choosing [company].

Sincerely,

[Your Name]
[Your Title]

[Company Letterhead]
[Company Name]
[Company Address]
[Company City, State, Zip]
[Company Phone/Fax/Website/E-mail]

[Date]

[First Name] [Last Name]
[Title]
[Company]
[Address]
[City], [State] [Zip]

Dear [Salutation]:

I want to thank you for giving me the opportunity the last time we talked to tell you about the advantages of using our marketing services. We're confident that our customized service will help you market your products and services effectively.

As you learned when we spoke recently, our marketing service offers you a number of beneficial features, including:

- product branding.

- developing a comprehensive online presence.

- launching new product awareness to the media and your customers.

- taking the steps to bring your business to the next level through innovative marketing.

I'd very much like to discuss how you can launch a comprehensive marketing plan in your business. I'll call your office on Wednesday, July 12, to make an appointment to meet with you. Thank you for your continued interest.

Sincerely,

[Your Name]
[Your Title]

[Company Letterhead]
[Company Name]
[Company Address]
[Company City, State, Zip]
[Company Phone/Fax/Website/E-mail]

[Date]

[First Name] [Last Name]
[Title]
[Company]
[Address]
[City], [State] [Zip]

Dear [Salutation]:

I appreciate the time that you gave us during our visit last week. Your staff is impeccable, dedicated, and enthusiastic.

We'll talk again after you've completed your review of our programs. Remember that we can save you more than next year on your system maintenance! That represents an unusual economy.

Again, thanks for the meeting and your kind consideration. I'll call you in two weeks.

Sincerely,

[Your Name]
[Your Title]

[Company Letterhead]
[Company Name]
[Company Address]
[Company City, State, Zip]
[Company Phone/Fax/Website/E-mail]

[Date]

[First Name] [Last Name]
[Title]
[Company]
[Address]
[City], [State] [Zip]

Dear [Salutation]:

I appreciate the time that you gave me during our telephone conversation today.

As you requested, here is the information about our payroll service. I call your attention to page seven of the white paper. You will see how three other companies of your size saved money by outsourcing their payroll processing to us.

It was a pleasure talking to you. Again, thanks for the telephone call and the consideration. I'll call you again in two weeks.

Sincerely,

[Your Name]
[Your Title]

ENCLOSURE

Follow-Up to a Meeting

[Company Letterhead]
[Company Name]
[Company Address]
[Company City, State, Zip]
[Company Phone/Fax/Website/E-mail]

[Date]

[First Name] [Last Name]
[Title]
[Company]
[Address]
[City], [State] [Zip]

Dear [Salutation]:

Thank you for taking the time to visit our showroom this past Tuesday.

I enjoyed meeting and talking with you regarding the custom cabinetry that you are considering adding to your office.

If you decide to proceed with your project, I would request a visit at your office to review the critical design elements with you. Our design services will ensure that the final product complements the existing interior of your office.

Thank you for considering us for this exciting project. If you have any questions or need additional information, please call. I look forward to hearing from you.

Sincerely,

[Your Name]
[Your Title]

[Company Letterhead]
[Company Name]
[Company Address]
[Company City, State, Zip]
[Company Phone/Fax/Website/E-mail]

[Date]

[First Name] [Last Name]
[Title]
[Company]
[Address]
[City], [State] [Zip]

Dear [Salutation]:

As I stated during our meeting on Wednesday, I am confident that we can provide the following material to you by mid-April of this year:

Customized design for D200 packaging and 10,000 units.

I estimate that the cost to you would be in the range of $12,000 to $14,000, including delivery expenses.

I would be pleased to provide you with a more detailed proposal once the final specifications are available from you.

I look forward to working with you on this project. Thanks once again for meeting with me on Wednesday.

Sincerely,

[Your Name]
[Your Title]

[Company Letterhead]
[Company Name]
[Company Address]
[Company City, State, Zip]
[Company Phone/Fax/Website/E-mail]

[Date]

[First Name] [Last Name]
[Title]
[Company]
[Address]
[City], [State] [Zip]

Dear [Salutation]:

I really enjoyed meeting you last Thursday at the Chamber Mixer.

As I mentioned, my firm offers some exclusive products that I'm sure you'd really enjoy. If you're interested in finding out more about our extensive cleaning supplies, give me a call at the office, and let's set up a time to meet. I'll be happy to take you through our catalog and tell you more about our extensive inventory.

I look forward to hearing from you.

Sincerely,

[Your Name]
[Your Title]

[Company Letterhead]
[Company Name]
[Company Address]
[Company City, State, Zip]
[Company Phone/Fax/Website/E-mail]

[Date]

[First Name] [Last Name]
[Title]
[Company]
[Address]
[City], [State] [Zip]

Dear [Salutation]:

It was a pleasure meeting you at the Charity Auction on Friday evening.

As I mentioned, my company offers professional payroll services. I am enclosing a brochure about our exclusive services.

If you're interested in learning more about our service, please give me a call at the office and let's set up a time to meet. I'll be happy to explain our service, and show you how you can save money by allowing us to take over your payroll processing.

I look forward to hearing from you.

Sincerely,

[Your Name]
[Your Title]

[Company Letterhead]
[Company Name]
[Company Address]
[Company City, State, Zip]
[Company Phone/Fax/Website/E-mail]

[Date]

[First Name] [Last Name]
[Title]
[Company]
[Address]
[City], [State] [Zip]

Dear [Salutation]:

I really enjoyed meeting you and hanging out at the block party on July 1.

When we exchanged cards, I think I mentioned that my business just added a new recruitment service for our current clients. I think it would really be great for you, especially because you do not have a full-time human resources director on staff.

Because you're planning to do some hiring this fall, you might want to set up a meeting so we can explain our service in more detail. Call me and let's find a convenient time in our schedules. I hope to see you again soon.

Sincerely,

[Your Name]
[Your Title]

[Company Letterhead]
[Company Name]
[Company Address]
[Company City, State, Zip]
[Company Phone/Fax/Website/E-mail]

[Date]

[First Name] [Last Name]
[Title]
[Company]
[Address]
[City], [State] [Zip]

Dear [Salutation]:

Thank you for meeting with me earlier today. I believe the time was well spent for both of us.

Within the next several days, you will receive a complete proposal from me. It will address all your concerns and needs. I am sure you will be quite pleased with the solution we can provide to your inventory control issues.

Thanks again for meeting with me. I look forward to working with you.

Sincerely,

[Your Name]
[Your Title]

Follow-Up to First Sale

[Company Letterhead]
[Company Name]
[Company Address]
[Company City, State, Zip]
[Company Phone/Fax/Website/E-mail]

[Date]

[First Name] [Last Name]
[Title]
[Company]
[Address]
[City], [State] [Zip]

Dear [Salutation]:

Thank you for your recent order of cleaning pool supplies. I trust your order has arrived and all the products meet your requirements.

You might be interested to know that we offer a maintenance contract for your commercial kitchen appliances. This spares your staff the task of weekly cleaning and ensures that your appliances are clean and ready for inspection by the county health department. Our maintenance contract usually includes a twice-weekly visit by one of our professional service people as well as all necessary cleaning supplies. The actual cost varies depending on the types of appliances, but it is usually about the same expense as performing the work yourself.

I will call you next week to see if you would like a free estimate.

Sincerely,

[Your Name]
[Your Title]

[Company Letterhead]
[Company Name]
[Company Address]
[Company City, State, Zip]
[Company Phone/Fax/Website/E-mail]

[Date]

[First Name] [Last Name]
[Title]
[Company]
[Address]
[City], [State] [Zip]

Dear [Salutation]:

You've reached our Valued Customer status. That's an honor to accorded only 5 percent of our customers.

It means that we recognize the special needs related to your volume. You automatically qualify for a 15-percent discount for all your purchases. Whenever you order supplies from our standard price list, you will automatically receive this discount.

We are also assigning you your very own customer service representative. Peggy Wilson will monitor your orders, review them, and make certain you are getting the best products and all appropriate discounts. Further, she will expedite your orders through our warehouse, making certain you are receiving priority processing. Her direct number is 555-5555.

Peggy will call you early next week to introduce herself. I'm sure you will enjoy working with her.

Be assured that I will continue to monitor your account personally. If there are ever any issues or concerns on your part, please call me immediately.

I appreciate your business.

Sincerely,

[Your Name]
[Your Title]

[Company Letterhead]
[Company Name]
[Company Address]
[Company City, State, Zip]
[Company Phone/Fax/Website/E-mail]

[Date]

[First Name] [Last Name]
[Title]
[Company]
[Address]
[City], [State] [Zip]

Dear [Salutation]:

It was a pleasure to process your first supplies order. I personally double-checked your order, and made certain it was shipped on a priority basis.

If there's anything I can ever do to help you, please do not hesitate to call me. I will stay in touch with you, making sure you receive both our updated price lists and sales bulletins.

Thank you once again for placing your first order with us.

Sincerely,

[Your Name]
[Your Title]

[Company Letterhead]
[Company Name]
[Company Address]
[Company City, State, Zip]
[Company Phone/Fax/Website/E-mail]

[Date]

[First Name] [Last Name]
[Title]
[Company]
[Address]
[City], [State] [Zip]

Dear [Salutation]:

Five days ago, I had the pleasure of filling your order. I would just like to thank you for purchasing your office supplies from us.

Labor Day isn't far away, and I think you may be interested in our sale that launches on September 5. It's our biggest event of the year—many items are available as buy-one-get-one specials.

I will send you a sales catalog as soon as they are available, and then follow up with you to see which items you want to order. It's a great time to stock up and save.

Sincerely,

[Your Name]
[Your Title]

Sales Letters to Customers

Selling to your current clients and customers always makes sense. They already know you, and the business relationship has been established. The idea for most enterprises is to sell more or different things to your customer or client base.

Staying in touch via sales letters is just part of the strategy. In addition to sales brochures, price lists, and other catalogs, sales letters allow you to create special messages to your clients. Use them to sell warranties, price clubs, service contracts, additional products, and other items to established customers.

Your messages to your customers can also include give aways and thank yous, while selling and pitching more products or services; and you can also ask for referrals from current customers.

Selling More to Current Customers

[Company Letterhead]
[Company Name]
[Company Address]
[Company City, State, Zip]
[Company Phone/Fax/Website/E-mail]

[Date]

[First Name] [Last Name]
[Title]
[Company]
[Address]
[City], [State] [Zip]

Dear [Salutation]:

Congratulations on your purchase of a new K-100 System during our recent winter sales campaign. I am sure you will be pleased with the performance.

Because of your smart decision to upgrade, you now qualify for our superior maintenance contract. I have enclosed our brochure that explains the program. If you have any questions, please call me.

Thanks again for your business.

Sincerely,

[Your Name]
[Your Title]

ENCLOSURE

[Company Letterhead]
[Company Name]
[Company Address]
[Company City, State, Zip]
[Company Phone/Fax/Website/E-mail]

[Date]

[First Name] [Last Name]
[Title]
[Company]
[Address]
[City], [State] [Zip]

Dear [Salutation]:

We've just become the exclusive state-wide dealer for EAPCO, a company that has been a respected manufacturer for nearly 30 years. Their specialty is top-quality, precision scales used in food preparation.

I believe their new K14A is a perfect fit for your packaging line. It is compatible with the sorter you purchased from us in April.

I'd like to show you a sample and review the specs with you and your engineering staff. Please check your calendar for on opening next Tuesday or Wednesday. I will be in touch to confirm.

Sincerely,

[Your Name]
[Your Title]

[Company Letterhead]
[Company Name]
[Company Address]
[Company City, State, Zip]
[Company Phone/Fax/Website/E-mail]

[Date]

[First Name] [Last Name]
[Title]
[Company]
[Address]
[City], [State] [Zip]

Dear [Salutation]:

This is not public information yet, so please keep this between us. I am pleased to inform you that next month, we will be offering a seasonal pool maintenance contract for commercial pools. Because you have used our repair services in the past, I thought you'd want to know about a new service we will be offering.

I will send you a brochure as soon as they are available. I'll be in touch.

Sincerely,

[Your Name]
[Your Title]

[Company Letterhead]
[Company Name]
[Company Address]
[Company City, State, Zip]
[Company Phone/Fax/Website/E-mail]

[Date]

[First Name] [Last Name]
[Title]
[Company]
[Address]
[City], [State] [Zip]

Dear [Salutation]:

We've received at least one order from you every year for several years. But as I look through our list of customers, I notice that you haven't ordered anything from us for the past 12 months.

I'm enclosing our recent sales flyer. Please notice all the great sports gear we have on sale. These are great items to include in a retail location such as yours.

I also enclosed an order form for your use. Just fax it to me with the quantities you want, and I'll process your order immediately.

If I can be of any assistance, please don't hesitate to call me at 555-5555.

Sincerely,

[Your Name]
[Your Title]

ENCLOSURE

[Company Letterhead]
[Company Name]
[Company Address]
[Company City, State, Zip]
[Company Phone/Fax/Website/E-mail]

[Date]

[First Name] [Last Name]
[Title]
[Company]
[Address]
[City], [State] [Zip]

Dear [Salutation]:

Thank you for ordering your new DL-350. I am sure that by now, you are using it, and finding it to be a great addition to your office.

I thought I'd alert you to a special offer: The sorter attachment for the DL-350 (the DL-355-A), is on sale this month only, or while our supplies last, for $550. That's 50 percent off.

Would you like to add the sorter to your new DL-355-A?

Call me at 555-5555 to place your order immediately.

Sincerely,

[Your Name]
[Your Title]

[Company Letterhead]
[Company Name]
[Company Address]
[Company City, State, Zip]
[Company Phone/Fax/Website/E-mail]

[Date]

[First Name] [Last Name]
[Title]
[Company]
[Address]
[City], [State] [Zip]

Dear [Salutation]:

Thank you for returning the service agreement for your main location. Your copy will be mailed to you within the next few days. It is on our vice president's desk, awaiting his signature.

In the interim, I thought I'd inquire as to whether you'd like a similar agreement for your Water Street location. We can offer the same service, discounted because of the second agreement. Please let me know if you'd like a formal proposal.

Thank you once again for your business.

Sincerely,

[Your Name]
[Your Title]

[Company Letterhead]
[Company Name]
[Company Address]
[Company City, State, Zip]
[Company Phone/Fax/Website/E-mail]

[Date]

[First Name] [Last Name]
[Title]
[Company]
[Address]
[City], [State] [Zip]

FOR CURRENT CUSTOMERS ONLY!

Dear [Salutation]:

Because of your recent (and first) order from us, you qualify for our special "customers only" sale. Next week, any order you place with us will be processed with a 10-percent discount.

To be sure you receive your discount, I will call you to see if you would like to place an order. If you do, I'll personally process it for you.

It is my pleasure to be your customer service representative. I appreciate your business.

Sincerely,

[Your Name]
[Your Title]

Selling Service Contracts to Current Customers

[Company Letterhead]
[Company Name]
[Company Address]
[Company City, State, Zip]
[Company Phone/Fax/Website/E-mail]

[Date]

[First Name] [Last Name]
[Title]
[Company]
[Address]
[City], [State] [Zip]

Dear [Salutation]:

The 120-day manufacturer's warranty on your D200 will expire next month. Don't lose any downtime by purchasing our service contract. Some of the features include:

◆ Priority Service—a professional technician guaranteed to be at your location within two hours of a service call.

◆ Routine Maintenance—a monthly maintenance visit to prevent downtime.

◆ Free loaner—if your D200 cannot be repaired within four hours, our technician will install a free loaner to keep your production on schedule.

Imagine: never more than four hours of downtime. The D200 is a machine, and machines do break. Protect yourself and your productivity by investing in our service contract.

I've enclosed a complete description for your review. Just sign and fax the agreement to me, and your service contract will go into place immediately after the manufacturer's warranty expires. If you have any questions, please call me.

Sincerely,

[Your Name]
[Your Title]

ENCLOSURE

[Company Letterhead]
[Company Name]
[Company Address]
[Company City, State, Zip]
[Company Phone/Fax/Website/E-mail]

[Date]

[First Name] [Last Name]
[Title]
[Company]
[Address]
[City], [State] [Zip]

Dear [Salutation]:

Thank you for using our service department. I noticed that you had called because of issues with your air conditioner. I am glad we were able to replace the capacitor and get your office cooled during the recent heat wave.

However, our technician commented that your system needs a complete inspection and some maintenance. Would like to schedule that service?

For your information, you could avoid the hassle of scheduling inspections, maintenance calls, and office-staff downtime. Consider a service contract with us. The service call would have been free; the only expense would have been the capacitor. It's amazing what a $7-part can do to office productivity. Our service contract would have prevented the loss of time you experienced, and paid for itself after the first hour of downtime.

I am enclosing a service contract agreement for your review. It can—and will—save you money.

Sincerely,

[Your Name]
[Your Title]

ENCLOSURE

Selling Price Clubs

[Company Letterhead]
[Company Name]
[Company Address]
[Company City, State, Zip]
[Company Phone/Fax/Website/E-mail]

[Date]

[First Name] [Last Name]
[Title]
[Company]
[Address]
[City], [State] [Zip]

Dear [Salutation]:

There is only one reason why you should join our Discount Price Club today: all your automotive supplies cost less. Expect discounts on tires, batteries, and all accessories—some items are even discounted at 5 or 10 percent. Others receive up to 20 percent off our regularly low prices.

You need to sign up to get the discount, so I've enclosed an application. For one full year, the cost of your membership is only $100. Most of our members earn back this membership fee within the first month.

If you have any questions, please call me.

Sincerely,

[Your Name]
[Your Title]

[Company Letterhead]
[Company Name]
[Company Address]
[Company City, State, Zip]
[Company Phone/Fax/Website/E-mail]

[Date]

[First Name] [Last Name]
[Title]
[Company]
[Address]
[City], [State] [Zip]

MEMBERSHIP HAS SPECIAL BENEFITS

Dear [Salutation]:

Did you know that if you become a member of our travel price club, you receive:

- 5-percent discount on cruises.

- free travel insurance (up to $2,500 per trip).

- complimentary 2-night stay at the Hotel Philadelphia, including one free gourmet meal.

- special pricing on European tours.

- discounted travel options on vacation packages.

- and much more!

Membership is only $125 per year. If you are going to travel during the next year, you can't afford not to become a member.

Sincerely,

[Your Name]
[Your Title]

Pitching With Give Aways

[Company Letterhead]
[Company Name]
[Company Address]
[Company City, State, Zip]
[Company Phone/Fax/Website/E-mail]

[Date]

[First Name] [Last Name]
[Title]
[Company]
[Address]
[City], [State] [Zip]

Dear [Salutation]:

COMPLIMENTARY TICKETS ENCLOSED

Here are two general admission tickets to the Greens—our local hometown minor league baseball stadium. They're good for the Friday, August 8th game.

It is just our way of thanking our favorite clients, and hopefully you'll think of us when you need to expand your parking lot.

Enjoy the game!

Sincerely,

[Your Name]
[Your Title]

ENCLOSURE

[Company Letterhead]
[Company Name]
[Company Address]
[Company City, State, Zip]
[Company Phone/Fax/Website/E-mail]

[Date]

[First Name] [Last Name]
[Title]
[Company]
[Address]
[City], [State] [Zip]

Dear [Salutation]:

We're doing it again.

Next [Day], [Date], we're offering our Internet Search Engine Optimization seminar. This information-packed seminar is vitally important to anyone that is using the Internet as part of their marketing plan.

I have reserved two complimentary seats for you. To attend, all you need to do is call and confirm them. Seating is limited—the only reason we are repeating the seminar is that so many wanted to attend, and could not because of space limitations.

Don't be left out. Call today to confirm your seats. I promise you will learn plenty in two hours about how to revitalize your Website! You will be glad you attended.

Sincerely,

[Your Name]
[Your Title]

[Company Letterhead]
[Company Name]
[Company Address]
[Company City, State, Zip]
[Company Phone/Fax/Website/E-mail]

[Date]

[First Name] [Last Name]
[Title]
[Company]
[Address]
[City], [State] [Zip]

FREE!

Dear [Salutation]:

Everyone likes something free! That's why we're sending you these free passes to annual business expo at the Champion Hall. There will be plenty of food and give aways!

When you're there, stop by our booth and look at the new display cases we offer retailers.

See you at the Expo.

Sincerely,

[Your Name]
[Your Title]

ENCLOSURE

Sending a Special Thank You

[Company Letterhead]
[Company Name]
[Company Address]
[Company City, State, Zip]
[Company Phone/Fax/Website/E-mail]

[Date]

[First Name] [Last Name]
[Title]
[Company]
[Address]
[City], [State] [Zip]

A SPECIAL THANK YOU!

Dear [Salutation]:

Just a quick note to thank you for your recent order! I am glad you have chosen us to provide safety vests to your crews.

We really do appreciate your business, and we look forward to serving you again in the future.

Sincerely,

[Your Name]
[Your Title]

[Company Letterhead]
[Company Name]
[Company Address]
[Company City, State, Zip]
[Company Phone/Fax/Website/E-mail]

[Date]

[First Name] [Last Name]
[Title]
[Company]
[Address]
[City], [State] [Zip]

Dear [Salutation]:

I cannot thank you enough for your trust and confidence in my company by referring Mary Smith. I look forward to assisting her now and in the future.

If I can be of any assistance to you and your company, please contact me.

Sincerely,

[Your Name]
[Your Title]

[Company Letterhead]
[Company Name]
[Company Address]
[Company City, State, Zip]
[Company Phone/Fax/Website/E-mail]

[Date]

[First Name] [Last Name]
[Title]
[Company]
[Address]
[City], [State] [Zip]

Dear [Salutation]:

Thank you for selecting us to provide vending service at your Park Country resort. We have ordered new machines, and installation will take place in two weeks, as per the agreement.

We are ready to provide additional service at your other location, too. We'd appreciate the opportunity of providing vending services to your guests at both locations.

Thank you once again for choosing us for your Park Country location.

Sincerely,

[Your Name]
[Your Title]

[Company Letterhead]
[Company Name]
[Company Address]
[Company City, State, Zip]
[Company Phone/Fax/Website/E-mail]

[Date]

[First Name] [Last Name]
[Title]
[Company]
[Address]
[City], [State] [Zip]

Dear [Salutation]:

We work hard to get customers like you, and often, in the bustle of doing business, we forget to say thank you. While it has been two weeks since you have placed your order, I do not want you to think that we do not appreciate and value your business.

Thank you very much for your order!

We hope you are pleased with the fast delivery and quality of the filters you ordered. We're ready to serve you again—and often!

Your business is very much appreciated—and be assured, we will do everything we can to earn all future business from you.

Sincerely,

[Your Name]
[Your Title]

[Company Letterhead]
[Company Name]
[Company Address]
[Company City, State, Zip]
[Company Phone/Fax/Website/E-mail]

[Date]

[First Name] [Last Name]
[Title]
[Company]
[Address]
[City], [State] [Zip]

Dear [Salutation]:

Thank you for recommending Mary Smith as a contact. I really appreciate the confidence you have placed in my company and in me.

Sincerely,

[Your Name]
[Your Title]

Seeking Referrals

[Company Letterhead]
[Company Name]
[Company Address]
[Company City, State, Zip]
[Company Phone/Fax/Website/E-mail]

[Date]

[First Name] [Last Name]
[Title]
[Company]
[Address]
[City], [State] [Zip]

Dear [Salutation]:

I really need your help. We have a sales contest, and I am trying to win. The only way I know that will work is to seek referrals from my customers.

Because we have a great relationship, I thought I'd ask if you know anyone I can contact who could use our current line of products?

I'd really appreciate any referrals you can provide. Thanks for your help.

Sincerely,

[Your Name]
[Your Title]

[Company Letterhead]
[Company Name]
[Company Address]
[Company City, State, Zip]
[Company Phone/Fax/Website/E-mail]

[Date]

[First Name] [Last Name]
[Title]
[Company]
[Address]
[City], [State] [Zip]

Dear [Salutation]:

Good clients like you are the lifeblood of our business. For more than three years, we have worked closely together, to our mutual benefit.

We are actively seeking referrals from our valued clients. Do you know anyone who you might recommend we contact? If so, would you please refer them to me?

Thank you for your consideration. I really appreciate it, and I look forward to a long and continued relationship with you and your company.

Sincerely,

[Your Name]
[Your Title]

Using Referrals

[Company Letterhead]
[Company Name]
[Company Address]
[Company City, State, Zip]
[Company Phone/Fax/Website/E-mail]

[Date]

[First Name] [Last Name]
[Title]
[Company]
[Address]
[City], [State] [Zip]

Dear [Salutation]:

Mr. John Johnson, president of Johnson Controls, Inc., recommended that I contact you. Mr. Johnson has been a customer of ours for the past three years. Throughout that time, Mr. Johnson has come to rely on us for all his financial services.

I have enclosed our latest brochure, which describes all the services we offer. I have also enclosed a special certificate, which allows you to use our online services free—and without any obligation—for the next 60 days.

I will call you next week to review our program, and answer any questions you might have. In the interim, if you need anything at all, please call me at (800) 555-5555.

I look forward to speaking with you, and introducing you further to our complete package of financial services.

Sincerely,

[Your Name]
[Your Title]

ENCLOSURE

[Company Letterhead]
[Company Name]
[Company Address]
[Company City, State, Zip]
[Company Phone/Fax/Website/E-mail]

[Date]

[First Name] [Last Name]
[Title]
[Company]
[Address]
[City], [State] [Zip]

Dear [Salutation]:

Mary Smith suggested I contact you as soon as she heard I was seeking employment. She speaks highly of you and your firm. Mary also said that she thought it would be a perfect match for both of us.

I am enclosing my resume for your review.

I would like to meet with you to discuss employment possibilities. I will be in your area next week, so I will call you this Friday to schedule a meeting.

I look forward to meeting you. Thank you for your consideration.

Sincerely,

[Your Name]
[Your Title]

[Company Letterhead]
[Company Name]
[Company Address]
[Company City, State, Zip]
[Company Phone/Fax/Website/E-mail]

[Date]

[First Name] [Last Name]
[Title]
[Company]
[Address]
[City], [State] [Zip]

Dear [Salutation]:

Sally Sandstone, a long-time customer and friend, encouraged me to contact you. Sally said you would likely be interested in our current line of products.

As you will see when you look through the enclosed catalog, we offer a complete array of display racks, cases, and solutions. More than 90 percent of the items in our catalog are in stock, and are shipped within 24 hours.

I am going to call later this week to see what your current or future needs may be. I will also have a special offer for you—a discount on your first order of $100 or more. I'll tell you more during our telephone call.

I look forward to speaking with you.

Sincerely,

[Your Name]
[Your Title]

Pitch Letters

Pitch letters are a bit different from sale letters. Pitches are fast swings, a quick attention-getter designed to get the attention of the letter reader. Short, tight, and concise pitch letters are a less-formal, but message-driven way to make contact with your letter reader.

Pitch letters should be approximately 100 words maximum, but can (and often should) be shorter.

Use these letters to pitch:

> ▷ price.

> ▷ service.

> ▷ reputation.

> ▷ a specific service.

> ▷ a special product.

Don't try to use a pitch letter to make a sale. Rather, the goal is to get the attention and develop the interest of the person receiving your letter.

Pitch Price

[Company Letterhead]
[Company Name]
[Company Address]
[Company City, State, Zip]
[Company Phone/Fax/Website/E-mail]

[Date]

[First Name] [Last Name]
[Title]
[Company]
[Address]
[City], [State] [Zip]

Dear [Salutation]:

We have the lowest prices on shipping supplies. Check us out at: *www.shippingforlessanywhere.com*.

Sincerely,

[Your Name]
[Your Title]

[Company Letterhead]
[Company Name]
[Company Address]
[Company City, State, Zip]
[Company Phone/Fax/Website/E-mail]

[Date]

[First Name] [Last Name]
[Title]
[Company]
[Address]
[City], [State] [Zip]

Dear [Salutation]:

The KL-1400, Franklin's Workhouse, is available now for only $8,950.*

Sincerely,

[Your Name]
[Your Title]

*This special price is good only for the first four KL-1400s ordered from our customers. When they are gone, the low price is, too!

[Company Letterhead]
[Company Name]
[Company Address]
[Company City, State, Zip]
[Company Phone/Fax/Website/E-mail]

[Date]

[First Name] [Last Name]
[Title]
[Company]
[Address]
[City], [State] [Zip]

Dear [Salutation]:

Don't delay! Order a new walk-in cooler this month—and receive a free two-year maintenance contract,* FREE!

But hurry—this offer expires in 15 days!

Sincerely,

[Your Name]
[Your Title]

* A $2,400 value!

[Company Letterhead]
[Company Name]
[Company Address]
[Company City, State, Zip]
[Company Phone/Fax/Website/E-mail]

[Date]

[First Name] [Last Name]
[Title]
[Company]
[Address]
[City], [State] [Zip]

LESS THAN $1 PER DAY!

Dear [Salutation]:

Each of your employees could be using our E-Z-Flow software—for less than $1 per day. At this low price, how can you afford not to install it on their computers?

I am sure you will save far more than $1 per day with increased productivity from each employee.

Let's place your order!

Sincerely,

[Your Name]
[Your Title]

[Company Letterhead]
[Company Name]
[Company Address]
[Company City, State, Zip]
[Company Phone/Fax/Website/E-mail]

[Date]

[First Name] [Last Name]
[Title]
[Company]
[Address]
[City], [State] [Zip]

LOCK IN FUEL COSTS TODAY

Dear [Salutation]:

What will fuel oil cost this winter?

Who knows?

But you can lock in your price today by signing a fuel oil delivery contract. Your price is guaranteed not to exceed the contracted amount. But hurry: this offer expires in 21 days—we must place our order with the refineries by June 15.

Don't be left out in the cold—or left to pay higher prices. Call us today!

Sincerely,

[Your Name]
[Your Title]

[Company Letterhead]
[Company Name]
[Company Address]
[Company City, State, Zip]
[Company Phone/Fax/Website/E-mail]

[Date]

[First Name] [Last Name]
[Title]
[Company]
[Address]
[City], [State] [Zip]

DO YOU NEED PROTECTIVE RAIN GEAR?

Dear [Salutation]:

My boss over-ordered, and for you, that's a good thing! We now offer discounts of 50 percent off our competitor's prices.

Here's a list of the items on sale. Be sure to look at page 3, under the Boots Section. I've never seen prices this low in the past 14 years.

These will move fast. Order today!

Sincerely,

[Your Name]
[Your Title]

ENCLOSURE

[Company Letterhead]
[Company Name]
[Company Address]
[Company City, State, Zip]
[Company Phone/Fax/Website/E-mail]

[Date]

[First Name] [Last Name]
[Title]
[Company]
[Address]
[City], [State] [Zip]

Dear [Salutation]:

A very special offer:

This Week Only!
KD-1400—Refurbished
50" Model
$2,595
2 Available.

The boss said, "get them sold." So we're notifying everyone that expressed interest in the KD-1400 in the past. The regular price is $4,850; this is a real savings! Call me if you have any questions.

Sincerely,

[Your Name]
[Your Title]

[Company Letterhead]
[Company Name]
[Company Address]
[Company City, State, Zip]
[Company Phone/Fax/Website/E-mail]

[Date]

[First Name] [Last Name]
[Title]
[Company]
[Address]
[City], [State] [Zip]

MEET THE AUTHOR!

Dear [Salutation]:

Save this date: March 16

George Sheldon, the author of *Sales & Pitch Letters for Busy People*, will be appearing in our booth from 4 to 6 p.m., to sign copies of his book.

We have a book reserved for you, too! Just bring along this letter and stop by our booth at the Expo.

See you then!

Sincerely,

[Your Name]
[Your Title]

[Company Letterhead]
[Company Name]
[Company Address]
[Company City, State, Zip]
[Company Phone/Fax/Website/E-mail]

[Date]

[First Name] [Last Name]
[Title]
[Company]
[Address]
[City], [State] [Zip]

HERE COMES THE EXPO AGAIN!

Dear [Salutation]:

It's that time of year—the Expo will be here in three weeks. If you are wondering what to do, be sure to stop by our booth! You can register to win a 60-inch big screen TV—as well as see all of this year's new barbecue grills on display.

Plus, there will be free food both days, too! There's no reason to be hungry at this year's Expo—unless you decide not to visit our booth.

See you at the Expo!

Sincerely,

[Your Name]
[Your Title]

Pitching for a Good Cause

[Company Letterhead]
[Company Name]
[Company Address]
[Company City, State, Zip]
[Company Phone/Fax/Website/E-mail]

[Date]

[First Name] [Last Name]
[Title]
[Company]
[Address]
[City], [State] [Zip]

Dear [Salutation]:

Your contribution last year has really helped us. Because of your support, we were able to:

1. [Project]

2. [Project]

3. [Project]

Will you help us again this year? We are facing many new challenges, including [New Project]. We really need your support.

Thank you for your kind consideration. I look forward to hearing from you.

Sincerely,

[Your Name]
[Your Title]

[Company Letterhead]
[Company Name]
[Company Address]
[Company City, State, Zip]
[Company Phone/Fax/Website/E-mail]

[Date]

[First Name] [Last Name]
[Title]
[Company]
[Address]
[City], [State] [Zip]

Dear [Salutation]:

I am inviting you and your company to join our community charity auction. The local auction is held on Labor Day, which supports Hospice Care. More than 2,500 people attend throughout the day. The event is traditionally covered by all local news media.

Would you like to be a part of this year's event? You can be a sponsor, a donor, or even volunteer at the auction.

It's easy to get involved. Just call me at [Phone] and we can discuss how you and your company can participate.

Your kind consideration is most appreciated.

Sincerely,

[Your Name]
[Your Title]

[Company Letterhead]
[Company Name]
[Company Address]
[Company City, State, Zip]
[Company Phone/Fax/Website/E-mail]

[Date]

[First Name] [Last Name]
[Title]
[Company]
[Address]
[City], [State] [Zip]

Dear [Salutation]:

Use the enclosed coupon and receive 15 percent off your purchase. Then you can judge for yourself about the quality of our products and delivery service.

Don't delay—the coupon expires October 31.

Sincerely,

[Your Name]
[Your Title]

Pitching Service

[Company Letterhead]
[Company Name]
[Company Address]
[Company City, State, Zip]
[Company Phone/Fax/Website/E-mail]

[Date]

[First Name] [Last Name]
[Title]
[Company]
[Address]
[City], [State] [Zip]

Dear [Salutation]:

Stop bogging yourself, and your staff, down with payroll processing! All you need to do is fax your payroll information to us 48 hours before you want the paychecks issued.

Let's talk!

Sincerely,

[Your Name]
[Your Title]

[Company Letterhead]
[Company Name]
[Company Address]
[Company City, State, Zip]
[Company Phone/Fax/Website/E-mail]

[Date]

[First Name] [Last Name]
[Title]
[Company]
[Address]
[City], [State] [Zip]

FASTEST SERVICE IN TOWN

Dear [Salutation]:

I know you could use our messenger service. We would move your packages from your location here in town to either Baltimore or Washington, in less time and for less money.

Try us! Judge for yourself and see if our service is not superior to what you are doing now.

Sincerely,

[Your Name]
[Your Title]

[Company Letterhead]
[Company Name]
[Company Address]
[Company City, State, Zip]
[Company Phone/Fax/Website/E-mail]

[Date]

[First Name] [Last Name]
[Title]
[Company]
[Address]
[City], [State] [Zip]

FASTER. EASIER. CHEAPER.

Dear [Salutation]:

We do title searches with 15 years of experience. When you need a title searched, call us. We'll turn around your search request within 24 hours. It will cost you less than you are paying now: only $33.50.

Sincerely,

[Your Name]
[Your Title]

[Company Letterhead]
[Company Name]
[Company Address]
[Company City, State, Zip]
[Company Phone/Fax/Website/E-mail]

[Date]

[First Name] [Last Name]
[Title]
[Company]
[Address]
[City], [State] [Zip]

DON'T FORGET THIS DATE: AUGUST 5

Dear [Salutation]:

The last day to order your window-cleaning service at last year's price is August 5. All service contracts issued after Aug. 5 are increasing by 8 percent.

SAVE NOW by returning the service contract mailed to you last week.

Sincerely,

[Your Name]
[Your Title]

[Company Letterhead]
[Company Name]
[Company Address]
[Company City, State, Zip]
[Company Phone/Fax/Website/E-mail]

[Date]

[First Name] [Last Name]
[Title]
[Company]
[Address]
[City], [State] [Zip]

Dear [Salutation]:

$78 or $122 per hour?

As a preferred customer, you can lock in a service rate of $78 rather than $122. But you can only do so if you become a preferred customer member. See the enclosed brochure for complete details.

Sincerely,

[Your Name]
[Your Title]

[Company Letterhead]
[Company Name]
[Company Address]
[Company City, State, Zip]
[Company Phone/Fax/Website/E-mail]

[Date]

[First Name] [Last Name]
[Title]
[Company]
[Address]
[City], [State] [Zip]

Dear [Salutation]:

We do windows (and doors, too). Check us out at:
www.todayswindowsandoors.com.

Sincerely,

[Your Name]
[Your Title]

P.S. If you decide to order our service, type in FG55 in the special offer box—you'll receive 15 percent off your first month!

Pitching Reputation

[Company Letterhead]
[Company Name]
[Company Address]
[Company City, State, Zip]
[Company Phone/Fax/Website/E-mail]

[Date]

[First Name] [Last Name]
[Title]
[Company]
[Address]
[City], [State] [Zip]

27 YEARS—AND WE'RE STILL HERE!

Dear [Salutation]:

How many computer consulting companies are still in business—at the same location—for 27 years?

Only us.

Maybe it's time for you to use the most reliable computer consulting company in the county.

Sincerely,

[Your Name]
[Your Title]

[Company Letterhead]
[Company Name]
[Company Address]
[Company City, State, Zip]
[Company Phone/Fax/Website/E-mail]

[Date]

[First Name] [Last Name]
[Title]
[Company]
[Address]
[City], [State] [Zip]

Dear [Salutation]:

We think we're one of the best, but the readers of *County Line* made it official: We were voted the number one appliance store in the state.

I've enclosed a reprint for your files; consider us for your next kitchen remodeling project.

Sincerely,

[Your Name]
[Your Title]

ENCLOSURE

[Company Letterhead]
[Company Name]
[Company Address]
[Company City, State, Zip]
[Company Phone/Fax/Website/E-mail]

[Date]

[First Name] [Last Name]
[Title]
[Company]
[Address]
[City], [State] [Zip]

Dear [Salutation]:

We never tried to be the cheapest, biggest, or loudest. We just tried to treat our customers fairly, and offer outstanding service for a reasonable price.

And if something goes wrong, we make it right. In 23 years of business, we haven't had one complaint filed against us. That's because we do not take our reputation in the community lightly.

If you want dependable plumbing and heating service for your rental units, call us.

Sincerely,

[Your Name]
[Your Title]

Pitching a Specific Service

[Company Letterhead]
[Company Name]
[Company Address]
[Company City, State, Zip]
[Company Phone/Fax/Website/E-mail]

[Date]

[First Name] [Last Name]
[Title]
[Company]
[Address]
[City], [State] [Zip]

NOW THERE IS NO REASON TO WAIT

Dear [Salutation]:

Have you been waiting to purchase the maintenance service you've always wanted? WAIT NO LONGER! We have a special deal for you!

For limited time only, you can use the enclosed coupon to get one FREE month of pool service for each month of pool service you purchase—for up to one year! Pay for six months—and get six months of service free!

It's a half-price deal you can afford. Need just two months of service? Pay for one month, and get the second month FREE!

Hurry! This offer expires next Friday.

Sincerely,

[Your Name]
[Your Title]

ENCLOSURE

[Company Letterhead]
[Company Name]
[Company Address]
[Company City, State, Zip]
[Company Phone/Fax/Website/E-mail]

[Date]

[First Name] [Last Name]
[Title]
[Company]
[Address]
[City], [State] [Zip]

STOP OVERPAYING

Dear [Salutation]:

You are probably paying too much for your bookkeeping service.

I can show you how you can pay less—much less—than you paying now. Let's meet, so I can show you how to save money each month.

Sincerely,

[Your Name]
[Your Title]

[Company Letterhead]
[Company Name]
[Company Address]
[Company City, State, Zip]
[Company Phone/Fax/Website/E-mail]

[Date]

[First Name] [Last Name]
[Title]
[Company]
[Address]
[City], [State] [Zip]

Dear [Salutation]:

Are you tired of overpaying for painting services?

With the latest equipment and trained technicians, we can do the job faster and for less than our competition.

May I bid on your next outside painting job?

Sincerely,

[Your Name]
[Your Title]

[Company Letterhead]
[Company Name]
[Company Address]
[Company City, State, Zip]
[Company Phone/Fax/Website/E-mail]

[Date]

[First Name] [Last Name]
[Title]
[Company]
[Address]
[City], [State] [Zip]

CITY FIRE DEPARTMENT CLOSING KITCHENS WITH DIRTY EXHAUST SYSTEMS

Dear [Salutation]:

The crackdown is underway. Don't get squeezed (or shut down)! Schedule an exhaust fan cleaning now.

Sincerely,

[Your Name]
[Your Title]

[Company Letterhead]
[Company Name]
[Company Address]
[Company City, State, Zip]
[Company Phone/Fax/Website/E-mail]

[Date]

[First Name] [Last Name]
[Title]
[Company]
[Address]
[City], [State] [Zip]

Dear [Salutation]:

Try our lawn treatment—only $29—this month only. Greener grass, and no weeds—just $29. Schedule your treatment today.

Sincerely,

[Your Name]
[Your Title]

P.S. Offer expires April 19.

Pitching a Special Product

[Company Letterhead]
[Company Name]
[Company Address]
[Company City, State, Zip]
[Company Phone/Fax/Website/E-mail]

[Date]

[First Name] [Last Name]
[Title]
[Company]
[Address]
[City], [State] [Zip]

15 PERCENT OFF NOW!

Dear [Salutation]:

You probably paid too much for your last major kitchen appliance.

How do I know? You didn't buy it from us.

It's time to get you into our show room now! And to get you in here, I've included a coupon good for a 15-percent discount on your order!

But hurry, because the coupon expires on August 15th!

Sincerely,

[Your Name]
[Your Title]

[Company Letterhead]
[Company Name]
[Company Address]
[Company City, State, Zip]
[Company Phone/Fax/Website/E-mail]

[Date]

[First Name] [Last Name]
[Title]
[Company]
[Address]
[City], [State] [Zip]

JUST ANNOUNCED!

Dear [Salutation]:

We are now an exclusive distributor of BELLSOFT, the leading non-profit management software.

In the next several days, I'll be sending you more information about the latest version of BELLSOFT, and a brochure describing how it can help your organization.

Sincerely,

[Your Name]
[Your Title]

[Company Letterhead]
[Company Name]
[Company Address]
[Company City, State, Zip]
[Company Phone/Fax/Website/E-mail]

[Date]

[First Name] [Last Name]
[Title]
[Company]
[Address]
[City], [State] [Zip]

Dear [Salutation]:

On sale this month: High-Back Microsuede Manager's Chair, Black—$99.

Regular price: $249.

Order now—offer good while supplies last, or until November 30.

Sincerely,

[Your Name]
[Your Title]

[Company Letterhead]
[Company Name]
[Company Address]
[Company City, State, Zip]
[Company Phone/Fax/Website/E-mail]

[Date]

[First Name] [Last Name]
[Title]
[Company]
[Address]
[City], [State] [Zip]

OVERSTOCKED!

Dear [Salutation]:

We have too many water coolers in our warehouse. So we're under orders to move them out. For current customers, they are only $35!

That's not a typo; $35 is all it takes to purchase a water cooler (get as many as you want). This offer includes free delivery, installation, and two free bottles of water for each cooler. Of course, we'll deliver water each week for you, too!

Order now! Call me at 555-5555.

Sincerely,

[Your Name]
[Your Title]

[Company Letterhead]
[Company Name]
[Company Address]
[Company City, State, Zip]
[Company Phone/Fax/Website/E-mail]

[Date]

[First Name] [Last Name]
[Title]
[Company]
[Address]
[City], [State] [Zip]

REFURBISHED LAPTOPS

Dear [Salutation]:

Only 20 Available—various sizes and types (different specs).

30 percent off to our customers that present this letter at the time of purchase. Available only in our showroom.

Sincerely,

[Your Name]
[Your Title]

[Company Letterhead]
[Company Name]
[Company Address]
[Company City, State, Zip]
[Company Phone/Fax/Website/E-mail]

[Date]

[First Name] [Last Name]
[Title]
[Company]
[Address]
[City], [State] [Zip]

FORGET THE SNOW AND ICE!

Dear [Salutation]:

Our annual boat show is just around the corner! And you are invited to a special preview!

The doors open to the public on Thursday, February 24 at 5 p.m. However, you can attend from 6 to 9 p.m., Wednesday February 23. It's a special sneak preview extended just to our past customers. I've enclosed four free passes for you. If you need more, call me.

I'll see you at the boat show!

Sincerely,

[Your Name]
[Your Title]

Special Sales, Pitch, and Marketing Documents

Sometimes, the purpose of a sales or pitch letter is get the reader to look at, read, or review other documents, materials, or even Websites. Most sales organizations create more than just sales letters as part of the sales process. Marketing brochures, white papers, special reports, and flyers are just some of the items that support the sales. Of course, none of these collateral materials are useful unless they are noticed and read by clients, prospects, or customers.

The idea is to pique your reader's interest. Try to get them interested—or hooked—and then hopefully they will move on to the other supporting documents.

Don't repeat what is in the other documents, but rather refer the letter reader to those documents. Keep them motivated by being brief and succinct.

[Company Letterhead]
[Company Name]
[Company Address]
[Company City, State, Zip]
[Company Phone/Fax/Website/E-mail]

[Date]

[First Name] [Last Name]
[Title]
[Company]
[Address]
[City], [State] [Zip]

Dear [Salutation]:

I am enclosing our latest white paper on automating the labeling process for custom manufacturing.

Please sure to read the section entitled, "Cost Savings by Proper Labeling."

You will be amazed at what small companies, such as yours, save each year by implementing this process.

If you have any questions, or need more information, please contact me.

Sincerely,

[Your Name]
[Your Title]

ENCLOSURE

[Company Letterhead]
[Company Name]
[Company Address]
[Company City, State, Zip]
[Company Phone/Fax/Website/E-mail]

[Date]

[First Name] [Last Name]
[Title]
[Company]
[Address]
[City], [State] [Zip]

END OF THE SEASON SALE

Dear [Salutation]:

Your filters are on sale—25 percent off if you buy 12 or more. See the enclosed sales brochure—I have highlighted the filters you use: see page 7.

Please let me know if you would like several cases at this discounted price.

Sincerely,

[Your Name]
[Your Title]

ENCLOSURE

[Company Letterhead]
[Company Name]
[Company Address]
[Company City, State, Zip]
[Company Phone/Fax/Website/E-mail]

[Date]

[First Name] [Last Name]
[Title]
[Company]
[Address]
[City], [State] [Zip]

Dear [Salutation]:

Did you receive our special sales catalog in last week's mail?

With these low prices, I thought for sure you'd be placing an order. Don't overlook the special discounts offered only one time each year!

Hurry! Sale ends in FOUR DAYS! Place your order today.

Sincerely,

[Your Name]
[Your Title]

[Company Letterhead]
[Company Name]
[Company Address]
[Company City, State, Zip]
[Company Phone/Fax/Website/E-mail]

[Date]

[First Name] [Last Name]
[Title]
[Company]
[Address]
[City], [State] [Zip]

Dear [Salutation]:

Our technical support staff has prepared a special report entitled, "Maintaining the Commercial Bakery."

It is 106 pages long. Of particular interest to you will be the recommended maintenance schedule, which begins on page 88. You can use this as a guide for your own preventative maintenance plans.

Would you like a complimentary copy?

Sincerely,

[Your Name]
[Your Title]

[Company Letterhead]
[Company Name]
[Company Address]
[Company City, State, Zip]
[Company Phone/Fax/Website/E-mail]

[Date]

[First Name] [Last Name]
[Title]
[Company]
[Address]
[City], [State] [Zip]

GET THE SCOOP EACH THURSDAY!

Dear [Salutation]:

Each Thursday, we issue an e-mail to our customers that have signed up for The Scoop. I'd recommend you subscribe, too.

It includes the latest additions to our product line and parts catalog. Also, it includes special sales information, and those items that are on sale. It often includes closeouts—items that will no longer be available, and are discounted for a quick sale.

Save money now by signing up for The Scoop! Visit our Website and click on The Scoop.

Sincerely,

[Your Name]
[Your Title]

[Company Letterhead]
[Company Name]
[Company Address]
[Company City, State, Zip]
[Company Phone/Fax/Website/E-mail]

[Date]

[First Name] [Last Name]
[Title]
[Company]
[Address]
[City], [State] [Zip]

Do You Need Tax Tips?

Dear [Salutation]:

A recent survey showed that more than half of local businesses are overpaying what they owe on their state taxes. Are you one of those businesses?

We are offering a free series of informational pamphlets explaining the most problematic issues. I am enclosing the first one of the series for your review.

If you would like to receive others, please complete the enclosed postcard and return it to me. I will see that you receive each of the pamphlets as they are released.

Sincerely,

[Your Name]
[Your Title]

PART IV
Incorporating Technology

E-mail, Faxes, and Other Electronic Delivery

The days of mass marketing by e-mail and fax are gone. The general rules are simple: If a prospect asks for information, you can deliver it. If you have an ongoing business relationship, you can probably market to that person via electronic delivery, but you'd be better off seeking permission before doing so.

Don't think that just because you created a great sales or pitch letter, now is the time to send as many messages as you can because you have the technology and skill to do so. That outlook could lead to huge problems.

Unsolicited Faxing

The Telephone Consumer Protection Act of 1991 prohibits the use of a telephone facsimile (fax) machine, computer, or other device to send an unsolicited advertisement (a "junk fax") to a fax machine. The Federal Communications Commission (FCC) enforces "junk" faxing; in so doing, the FCC issued public information about sending unsolicited commercial faxes. In summary, the Telephone Consumer Protection Act (TCPA) and the FCC rules generally prohibit most unsolicited fax advertisements.

In addition, the Junk Fax Prevention Act, passed by Congress in 2005, directs the FCC to amend its rules adopted pursuant to the TCPA regarding fax advertising. According to the FCC, the revised rules include:

> ⊳ Codify an established business relationship (EBR) exemption to the prohibition on sending unsolicited fax advertisements.

> ⊳ Define EBR for unsolicited fax advertisements.

> ⊳ Require the sender of the fax advertisements to provide specified notice and contact information on the fax that allows recipients to "opt-out" of any future faxes from the sender.

> ⊳ Specify the circumstances under which a request to "opt-out" complies with the Act.

According to the FCC, to "understand the revised rules, you must first understand the meaning of the terms 'unsolicited advertisement' and 'established business relationship.'" As defined in FCC rules, an "unsolicited advertisement" is "any material advertising the commercial availability or quality of any property, goods, or services which is transmitted to any person without that person's prior express invitation or permission, in writing or otherwise."

The definition continues. The FCC says "an 'established business relationship' or EBR is a prior or existing relationship formed by a voluntary two-way communication between a person or entity and a business or residential subscriber with or without an exchange of consideration [payment], on the basis of an inquiry, application, purchase or transaction by the business or residential subscriber regarding products or services offered by such person or entity, which relationship has not been previously terminated by either party."

The FCC recently expanded its junk fax rules. It issued an "Amended Fax Rules and Established Business Relationship Exemption."

The rules provide that it is unlawful to send unsolicited advertisements to any fax machine, including those at both businesses and residences, without the recipient's prior express invitation or permission. Fax advertisements, however, may be sent to recipients with whom the sender has an EBR, as long as the fax number was provided voluntarily by the recipient. Specifically, a fax advertisement may be sent to an EBR customer if the sender also:

> ▷ obtains the fax number directly from the recipient, through, for example, an application, contact information form, or membership renewal form.

> ▷ obtains the fax number from the recipient's own directory, advertisement, or site on the Internet, unless the recipient has noted on such materials that it does not accept unsolicited advertisements at the fax number in question.

> ▷ has taken reasonable steps to verify that the recipient consented to have the number listed, if obtained from a directory or other source of information compiled by a third party.

Fax Broadcasters

There are companies that provide fax-broadcasting services. These companies will send a fax to your list, or to a list of fax numbers it has prepared. According to the FCC, you are responsible even if you hired a fax broadcasting company. "Generally, the person or business on whose behalf a fax is sent or whose property, goods, or services are advertised is liable for a violation of the junk fax rules, even if the person or business did not physically send the fax," the FCC says. "A fax broadcaster also may be liable if it has a high degree of involvement in the sender's fax message, such as supplying the fax numbers to which the message is sent, providing a source of fax numbers, making representations about the legality of faxing to those numbers, or advising about how to comply with the junk fax rules. Also, if a fax broadcaster is highly involved in the sender's fax messages, the fax broadcaster must provide its name on the fax."

Opt-Out Notice Requirements

The FCC requires opt-out notices on all faxes. According to the FCC, "Senders of permissible fax advertisements (those sent under an EBR or with the recipient's prior express permission) must provide notice and contact information on the fax that allows recipients to opt-out of future faxes. The notice must:

> ▷ be clear and conspicuous on the first page of the advertisement.

> ▷ state that the recipient may make a request to the sender not to send any future faxes, and that failure to comply with the request within 30 days is unlawful.

> ▷ include a telephone number, fax number, and cost-free mechanism (including a toll-free telephone number, local number for local recipients, toll-free fax number, Website address, or e-mail address) to opt-out of faxes. These numbers and cost-free mechanism must permit consumers to make opt-out requests 24 hours a day, seven days a week. Senders who receive a request not to send further faxes that meet the requirements listed in the next section must honor that request within the shortest reasonable time from the date of the request, not to exceed 30 days. They are also prohibited from sending future fax advertisements to the recipient unless the recipient subsequently provides prior express permission to the sender."

Violations and Penalties

The FCC does issue warning citations and imposes fines against companies violating or suspected of violating the junk fax rules, but does not award individual damages. In addition to complaining to the FCC, an individual can file TCPA-related complaints with state authorities, including local or state consumer protection offices or the state Attorney General's office.

Anyone receiving junk faxes can also bring a private suit against the violator in an appropriate court. Through a private suit, the person receiving the fax can either recover the actual monetary loss that resulted from the TCPA violation, or receive up to $500 in damages for each violation, whichever is greater. The law also allows the court to triple the damages for each violation if it finds that the defendant willingly or knowingly committed the violation. Filing a complaint with the FCC or other government regulator does not prevent the filing of a suit in a local court.

The fax itself will be the primary evidence used against the person sending the fax.

Fax Marketing or Selling

Clearly, the law prohibits mass fax marketing, except to those individuals, companies, or businesses where you already have an established business relationship. Your best practice it to request permission to send the fax. Don't just gather fax numbers and begin transmitting sales messages—each fax sent to an individual fax number could cost you $1,500 in penalties!

Sending Unsolicited Commercial E-Mail

Just as bulk faxing is no longer permitted, bulk e-mailing is also illegal. The CAN-SPAM Act of 2003 (Controlling the Assault of Non-Solicited Pornography and Marketing Act) establishes requirements for those who send commercial e-mail. Unsolicited Commercial E-mail (often called UCE, or more popular, spam), is sent by the hundreds of thousands by professional spammers (people or companies that send spam). The CAN-SPAM Act spells out penalties for spammers and companies whose products are advertised in spam if they violate the law, and gives consumers the right to have mass e-mailers to stop spamming them.

The law became effective January 1, 2004. It covers e-mail whose primary purpose is advertising or promoting a commercial product or service, including content on a Website.

According to the FTC, "A 'transactional or relationship message,' or e-mail that facilitates an agreed-upon transaction or updates a customer in an existing business relationship, may not contain false or misleading routing information, but otherwise is exempt from most provisions of the CAN-SPAM Act."

The Federal Trade Commission (FTC), the nation's consumer protection agency, is authorized to enforce the CAN-SPAM Act. CAN-SPAM also gives the Department of Justice (DOJ) the authority to enforce its criminal sanctions. Other federal and state agencies can enforce the law against organizations under their jurisdiction, and companies that provide Internet access may sue violators, as well.

What the Law Requires

According to the FTC, here is a rundown of the law's main provisions:

> ⊳ It bans false or misleading header information. Your e-mail's "From," "To," and routing information—including the originating domain name and e-mail address—must be accurate and identify the person who initiated the e-mail.

▷ It prohibits deceptive subject lines. The subject line cannot mislead the recipient about the contents or subject matter of the message.

▷ It requires that your e-mail give recipients an opt-out method. You must provide a return e-mail address or another Internet-based response mechanism that allows a recipient to ask you not to send future e-mail messages to that e-mail address, and you must honor the requests. You may create a "menu" of choices to allow a recipient to opt out of certain types of messages, but you must include the option to end any commercial messages from the sender.

▷ Any opt-out mechanism you offer must be able to process opt-out requests for at least 30 days after you send your commercial e-mail. When you receive an opt-out request, the law gives you 10 business days to stop sending e-mail to the requestor's e-mail address. You cannot help another entity send e-mail to that address, or have another entity send e-mail on your behalf to that address. Finally, it's illegal for you to sell or transfer the e-mail addresses of people who choose not to receive your e-mail, even in the form of a mailing list, unless you transfer the addresses so another entity can comply with the law.

▷ It requires that commercial e-mail be identified as an advertisement and include the sender's valid physical postal address. Your message must contain clear and conspicuous notice that the message is an advertisement or solicitation and that the recipient can opt out of receiving more commercial e-mail from you. It also must include your valid physical postal address.

The fines for violations are substantial, according to the FTC.

Each violation of the law's provisions is subject to fines of up to $11,000. Deceptive commercial e-mail also is subject to laws banning false or misleading advertising. Additional fines are provided for commercial e-mailers who not only violate the rules described previously, but also:

- "harvest" e-mail addresses from Websites or Web services that have published a notice prohibiting the transfer of e-mail addresses for the purpose of sending e-mail.

- generate e-mail addresses using a "dictionary attack"— combining names, letters, or numbers into multiple permutations.

- use scripts or other automated ways to register for multiple e-mail or user accounts to send commercial e-mail.

- relay e-mails through a computer or network without permission; for example, by taking advantage of open relays or open proxies without authorization.

The law allows the DOJ to seek criminal penalties, including imprisonment, for commercial e-mailers who do—or conspire to:

- use another computer without authorization and send commercial e-mail from or through it.

- use a computer to relay or retransmit multiple commercial e-mail messages to deceive or mislead recipients or an Internet access service about the origin of the message.

- falsify header information in multiple e-mail messages and initiate the transmission of such messages.

- register for multiple e-mail accounts or domain names using information that falsifies the identity of the actual registrant.

- falsely represent themselves as owners of multiple Internet Protocol addresses that are used to send commercial e-mail messages.

Clearly, the penalties are substantial. Don't create a terrific sales message and begin sending to any e-mail address you can locate. Each e-mail could cost you $11,000, and certainly plenty of adverse publicity. And don't even consider any scheme that would "mask" your e-mail. Getting caught doing so is just not worth it, not matter what it is that you are offering for sale.

Using Mail Merge, Contact Managers, and Other Automated Systems

Today's computerized world makes it much easier to write, create, and deliver sales letters. While word processing software is used to create the letters, both in content and style, contact managing software allows you to access your customers, clients, and prospects from a predesigned database.

You can create your own contact manager system with a word processor file or a spreadsheet. Some use a custom designed database, while others use a contact and customer manager application, such as ACT!, GoldMine, or Microsoft's Business Contact Manager in conjunction with Outlook. There are many other types of programs, too. Larger sales operations use Customer Relationship Management software, often called CRM. There are many different types of software packages marketed and deployed throughout the country.

As you have learned throughout this book, the more customized you can make a sales or pitch letter, the more likely it will be well-received. You've also learned that you should not just mass produce sales letters and send them in a shotgun approach, hoping to hit someone.

Although you can inexpensively mass e-mail or mass fax to prospects, in most cases, you are probably breaking the law. (See Chapter 13 for more information, or check out the Federal Communications Website at *www.fcc.gov* and the Federal Trade Commission's Website at *www.ftc.gov*.) Don't be tempted to do it, just because you can.

Rather than use a contact manager or mail merge feature to mass-produce a sales letter for hundreds of contacts, work your list to customize your message. Consider these two examples:

[Company Letterhead]
[Company Name]
[Company Address]
[Company City, State, Zip]
[Company Phone/Fax/Website/E-mail]

[Date]

[First Name] [Last Name]
[Title]
[Company]
[Address]
[City], [State] [Zip]

Dear [Salutation]:

Thank you for your recent order. We really appreciate your business. If you ever have any questions or need more information, please contact me.

Sincerely,

[Your Name]
[Your Title]

[Company Letterhead]
[Company Name]
[Company Address]
[Company City, State, Zip]
[Company Phone/Fax/Website/E-mail]

[Date]

[First Name] [Last Name]
[Title]
[Company]
[Address]
[City], [State] [Zip]

Dear [Salutation]:

Thank you for your recent order on January 18 for 12 × 18 × 24 white package containers. Our records indicate your order was delivered January 19, and a follow-up call was made to your packaging supervisor, Bonnie Clark, three days later, just to make sure they met your specifications.

We really appreciate your business, and we would be happy to supply you with more package containers. We have a huge inventory of all sizes and styles. I am enclosing several catalog sheets for your files and future reference.

If you ever have any questions or need more information about our complete line of package containers, please contact me directly at extension 112, or via e-mail at name@email.com.

We want to be your vendor of choice. Thank you, once again, [Name], for this order. We hope it is the beginning of a new and long-lasting business relation with you and [Company].

Sincerely,

[Your Name]
[Your Title]

ENCLOSURE

As you can see from the second example, there is much more specific information about the customer included in the body of the letter. This type of information is easily extracted in most contact manager software applications.

It may take some planning of your letters, and the data fields, to get this information properly placed in your final sales letter. The data fields must be maintained and obviously updated. Often, that can be automated, or completed manually. Without proper planning or insertion, your final letter can be unusable, or if used, sent with mistakes.

The goal is to create a letter that never looked as though it was assembled from a mail merge or contact manager program. Rather, its appearance should look as though you spent time and to create a special letter to your client or prospect.

It doesn't matter what type of software you are using but, instead, you should master it to produce the best possible sales or pitch letter. In addition to creating the correspondence within your software, you can also keep track of your customers and clients. You can easily decide what the next course of action/contact is, and when. On a specific date, you are reminded to contact that customer or prospect.

All of these factors are important in your letters, whether they are for selling or pitching. Using all of the information in this book, as well as good old fashioned practicing, will develop your skills, and eventually make you a successful sales and pitch writer.

Index

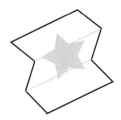

About the Author

GEORGE SHELDON is the author of more than 30 books. He has been writing sales and pitch letters for more than 25 years as part of his freelancing business.

In addition to writing about history and business, George is an active photographer. He uses his sales and pitch letters and sell his photography to stock agencies, art representatives, and numerous clients. His pitch and sales letters are sent worldwide.

George lives in Lancaster, Pennsylvania.

In order to use this CD properly, please open the Word file labeled "Table of Contents Complete" first.

This file contains both a Table of Contents for the CD's Exclusive Letters, as well as a Table of Contents for the letters from the book.

Each letter on this CD is hyperlinked from the Table of Contents, and can be reached by clicking the proper link in the Table of Contents Complete file.

If you wish to access only the CD Exclusive Letters, they can be accessed from either the Table of Contents Complete File, or through the "Table of Contents CD Only" File.

All letters can be read as individual files, or found through the Table of Contents.

OTHER GREAT *LETTER WRITING* BOOKS
BY CAREER PRESS

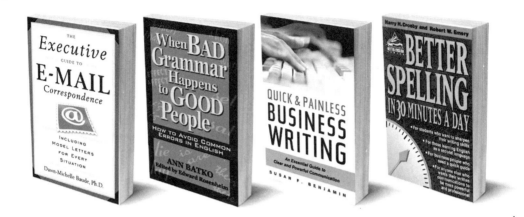

Business Letters for Busy People
Fourth Edition (w/CD)
Edited by John A. Carey
EAN 978-1-56414-612-0

Everyday Letters for Busy People
Revised Edition
Deborah Hart May and Regina
McAloney
EAN 978-1-56414-712-7

**The Encyclopedia of Business
Letters, Fax Memos, and E-Mail**
Robert W. Bly
EAN 978-1-56414-375-4

**The Executive Guide to E-Mail
Correspondence**
Including Model Letters for Every
Situation
Dawn-Michelle Baude, Ph.D.
EAN 978-1-56414-910-7

Quick & Painless Business Writing
An Essential Guide to Clear and Powerful
Communication
Susan F. Benjamin
EAN 978-1-56414-900-8

When Bad Grammar Happens to Good People
How to Avoid Common Errors in English
Ann Batko and Edited by Edward Rosenheim
EAN 978-1-56414-722-6

Better Grammar in 30 Minutes a Day
Constance Immel and Florence Sacks
EAN 978-1-56414-204-7

Better Sentence Writing in 30 Minutes a Day
Dianna Campbell
EAN 978-1-56414-203-0

Better Spelling in 30 Minutes a Day
Harry H. Crosby and Robert W. Emery
EAN 978-1-56414-202-3

**AVAILABLE WHEREVER BOOKS ARE SOLD,
OR CALL 201-848-0310**

careerpress.com

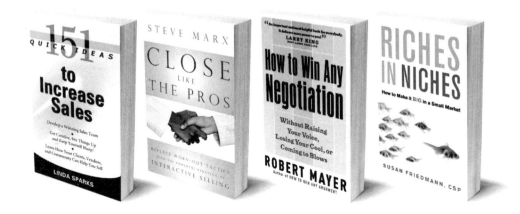